Poems for the Writing:
Prompts for Poets

Second Edition

Poems for the Writing: Prompts for Poets

Second Edition

by Valerie Fox and Lynn Levin

Illustrated by Don Riggs

2019
Texture Press
Norman, Oklahoma

Poems for the Writing: Prompts for Poets, Second Edition
Copyright © 2019 by Valerie Fox and Lynn E. Levin
All rights reserved
Illustrations copyright © 2019 by Donald Riggs
All rights reserved

Texture Press
1108 Westbrooke Terrace
Norman, OK 73072
Managing Editor: Susan Smith Nash, Ph.D.
www.texturepress.org

ISBN: 978-1-945784-08-8
Library of Congress Control Number: 2019904610

Cover design: Arlene Ang
Cover art: *Handwriting* by Christine Hamm
Book design: Texture Press

Afterwards, I was still stomping on the brake—Christopher Bursk

CONTENTS

ACKNOWLEDGEMENTS

We are deeply grateful to our publisher, Susan Smith Nash, for helping to conceive of this book and for supporting it with her wisdom and kindness. We thank Arlene Ang for her editing expertise. Applause to Don Riggs for illustrating the book. Special thanks also to Meg Pokrass and Kirsten Kaschock for helping us develop chapters.

INTRODUCTION

Welcome to the second edition of *Poems for the Writing: Prompts for Poets*. Our book began with the aim of helping both novice and working poets find engaging and unusual ways to tell their stories, express their memories, share their observations, and weave in bits and pieces from their reading. We also began with the premise that all of our prompts—in order to earn a place in the book—must be extensively classroom and workshop tested. Only the most effective, productive, and inspiring prompts earn a place in *Poems for the Writing: Prompts for Poets*. We saw the positive response to our first edition and, eager to make a good thing even better, we developed six new prompts and collected a wealth of examples of poems written to the new prompts and to the previous ones. Our example poems are written by undergrads, poets in community workshops, and working poets.

Our prompts serve as doorknobs and doors, providing torque and entry points that help writers flow their experiences and new techniques into their poems and writing process. The doorknob and door metaphor harkens to our first prompt, the paraclausithyron, a lover's lament before a closed door. We like to think that the second edition of *Poems for the Writing: Prompts for Poets* will open many new doors for you.

What is new in this book

Our six new prompts invite poets to imagine an encounter with an admired person, offer gratitude, stand at a crossroads and describe the goings-on, muse about how life might have been different had an action been taken or not taken, dream of being a superhero, and build a poem by incorporating song titles.

We also invite writers to explore the possibilities of boundary-jumping genres that might combine the prose poem with flash fiction or the prose poem with the list poem. We encourage writers to experiment with various rhetorical strategies: incorporating pieces of found text such as street signs and song titles, listing fanciful instructions, using math and counting approaches, and, in the case of the bibliomancy prompt, selecting quotations and facts from reference works. Some of the prompts pose physical or meditative situations.

Some of the prompts and examples show how poems may wander into surrealistic and dream territory. On the other hand, many of our prompts are stalwarts in the lyrical and narrative tradition.

We sought to feature prompts and example writings that are comic and serious, retro and contemporary, challenging without being too heady or difficult. In short, we want to communicate our approach to teaching and craft, which is friendly, open, and even eclectic.

Our contributors are more diverse than ever. Here you will find poets from a range of ages, from many ethnicities and cultural backgrounds, new poets and noted poets. While most of our contributors are from the US, we also include work from writers living in Canada, Australia, the UK, Israel, and Brazil, as well as poets from the tradition: Shakespeare, Emily Dickinson, and Paul Laurence Dunbar.

Convenient and easy-to-navigate, our new edition features a new chapter format that groups the prompt instructions with the example poems. Meander through the book to find the prompts that appeal to you.

We have always believed that writers from all walks of life have within them the ability to compose poems worth writing and worth reading. If you are a student writer—as many of our contributors are—we hope that this book will usher you into new poetic possibilities. If you are a working poet—as many of our contributors are—we hope you will find these prompts unique, inviting, and even provocative. If you are a creative writing teacher or workshop leader—as many of our users are—we are confident that you will find here a wealth of lesson plans and many doors through which you may guide your students toward a love of poetry and a love of writing of poems. We wish you well in your poetic journeys.

With our very best,

V. F. and L. L.
Philadelphia, Pennsylvania

To our contributors who tried the prompts and found them worthy of their poetic attentions, we extend our immeasurable gratitude.

1.
Paraclausithyron

At one time or another, you may have had the unpleasant situation of being shut out of something: a business meeting, a party, a conversation, or your sweetheart's apartment or bedroom.

There's a poem for that: the paraclausithyron.

The paraclausithyron, a motif which originated in Greek and Roman poetry, expresses a lover's lament before the beloved's closed door. The lover, often speaking at night, pleads entry. His or her tone may be seductive, cajoling, angry, comic, rowdy, drunken, desperate, or a combination of any of those things. Some of the best known paraclausithyra come from the Latin poets. In *The Art of Love* (Book One: VI), Ovid's speaker cries out to a gatekeeper in the dark of night and begs him to open the gate just enough to let him slip in to visit his lady. Horace, on the other hand, takes a rather threatening approach in his paraclausithyron "To Lycia" (*Odes,* Book Three: X). Instead of sweet-talking Lycia into opening her door, Horace first tells her that she could do a lot worse than to have him as a lover. Then he insults her virtue, calls her cold-hearted, and warns her—while standing in her garden on a freezing night—that there's a limit to his patience.

Write your own lament before a closed door. Your paraclausithyron may be spooky, ardent, funny, apologetic, hopeless, or optimistic. Your speaker may even succeed in gaining entry.

Am I bothering you?—Alina Macneal

Alina Macneal

WINTER GIRLFRIEND

Is my knocking too loud,
too insistent?
Am I bothering you?
Sorry…I'll go away, if you want me to.
It's just that I was hoping to…you know…come in.
I brought you a soy macchiato from the Planet
and it's, like, tepid by now.
Are you in the shower or something?
Or running the garbage disposal?
I was in the neighborhood and thought that
we could, like, talk, and then lie down
on your sofa, under the orange afghan
like we used to in February and,
you know, make out.

The forsythia bush outside your door
is yellow, and the daffodils are glowing in the sun.
You loved me in the wind and cold.
Isn't this an even better time for love?

Or have you moved on to a
springtime girlfriend
into whose new ear
you're pouring old endearments?
Is it that Ashtanga girl from Studio Baobab?
I feel so pathetic standing here.
On a day like this
I should be jogging
or cleaning my clothes closet,
not begging a useless man like you
for a drop of affection.
Stupid door!
How often I knocked on your frosted pane

and turned the icy door knob.
Have you forgotten me too
now that sunshine kisses your face?

Lynn Levin

PARACLAUSITHYRON

The ice upon the hyacinth
the black antennae of the clock
are not as cruel as the door
you shut against me.
I beg news of your dreams
the milk of your voice.
Don't waste yourself
like an unread book
hoarding your wisdom and charm
or keep yourself boxed up
like a hat too fine to get a little soiled.
Sooner or later
your joints will rust
like the hinges of this door,
everything will become harder
and harder to open.
I will wait a year, maybe two
then don't blame me if I seek
someone simpler
less in need of coaxing.

Emily Dickinson

I YEARS HAD BEEN FROM HOME (#609)

I Years had been from Home
And now before the Door
I dared not enter, lest a Face
I never saw before

Stare solid into mine
And ask my Business there –
"My Business but a Life I left
Was such remaining there?"

I leaned upon the Awe –
I lingered with Before –
The Second like an Ocean rolled
And broke against my ear –

I laughed a crumbling Laugh
That I could fear a Door
Who Consternation compassed
And never winced before.

I fitted to the Latch
My Hand, with trembling care
Lest back the awful Door should spring
And leave me in the Floor –

Then moved my Fingers off
As cautiously as Glass
And held my ears, and like a Thief
Fled gasping from the House –

2.
Fibonacci Poem

Write a poem based on the Fibonacci sequence: 0, 1, 1, 2, 3, 5, 8, 13, 21, 34, 55, 89, 144 (and so on). The series is formed by adding the last two terms to create each subsequent term: $0+1=1$, $1+1=2$, $1+2=3$, $2+3=5$, etc.

The Fibonacci sequence, named after the most important European mathematician of the Middle Ages, Leonardo of Pisa, also known as Leonardo Fibonacci, has been called nature's numbering system. Fibonacci studied books by Indian mathematicians who were already discussing the pattern that later came to be known as the Fibonacci sequence. Fibonacci was trying, or so the story goes, to solve a problem about rabbits after a number of generations.

Basing a poem on the Fibonacci sequence may lead to unexpected insights in the way that following a traditional form like the sestina or villanelle might also do. The beauty and symmetry of the series and, indeed, other sequences may lead to beauty and symmetry in your poem. The influence of the numbers series on the finished poem or the procedures of the poet may or may not be obvious to readers.

A whole group might write or, at least, begin a collaborative Fibonacci poem. One person might write the first line, another the second line that pays off from the first, and so on. Poets with an affinity for this prompt (or for counting and numbers) will devise ingenious ways to craft the Fibonacci poem.

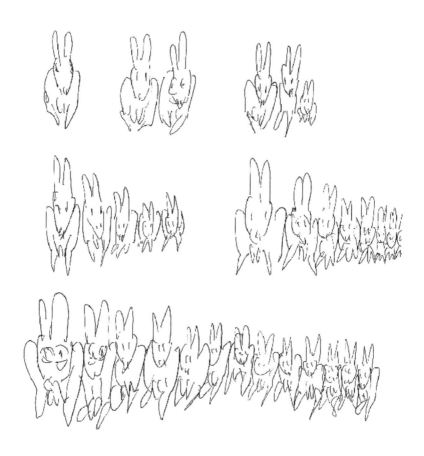

What is our number?—Peter Wood

Don Riggs

THAT'S THE WAY IT GOES

Each new year is a smaller fraction of your life.
—Mr. Gallagher, high school math teacher

First we have no age at all. Then we're one.
In another year we turn two, then three,
as our stumbling gets a bit steadier.
Suddenly, we are five, an entire hand
that we look at in wonder. Let's skip
the first few grades, because when we are eight
we have begun to discover novels
on library shelves, and not long after
we're teens. Then old enough to drink, which we
do on that first opportunity. The
hangover lasts until we're 34,
which is not quite time for midlife crises,
though some manage. 55 is one's prime
but, we know then we'll soon be 89.

Peter Wood

FIBONACCI POEM

Oh

I,

I

And you

Do we count?

What is our number?

And how did it come to be this

Most unfortunate of numbers, the dreaded thirteen?

And passing that, we are here beyond the scope of lines, counting our breath and breathing deep,

At last arriving, haven't we, at a place calling for the rolling cadences Walt Whitman charged against the tyranny of numbers?

Have you, like Fibonacci, seen a simple thread spin out and bind? I have seen thread spin out and bind the branching leaves of licorice, the spiral seeds in a sunflower's head, the spider to the nebulae, the cancer to a brain.

Luray Gross

FIBONACCI REVERIE

Familiar emptiness.

Then the apparition
of a glass half empty,
another half full. Both
swept to the floor.

Three cards in the hand,
five under the table.
In the sober church on the hill,
a double string quartet, eight bows sawing away.

Thirteen donuts, cookies, ears of corn—
whatever the person behind the counter, baker or not,
decides to drop into the bag.

Under the basket, who's first to reach 21?

Thirty-four and pregnant, I lie on the floor
and gather our cranky firstborn into my arms,
settle her on my chest and belly. We sleep
while the child still hidden kicks and tumbles.

Fifty-five bottles of beer on the wall, fifty-five bottles of beer
my mother, who likely never sipped from even one,
sang as she steered the station wagon with one hand,
wagged the fingers of the other to the broken-record tune.

I suppose I could keep the sequence going,
counting and naming, naming and counting
geese lifting from the field, cars before me at the toll booth,
bubbles before they break.
This morning, a single jet arrowed west toward clear blue,

away from the ranks of graypink clouds, through which the one sun
began to rise. Clouds too many to count, I took the time to think,
thinking too of calendar photos—Arizona canyons lit by slanting sun,
one beyond the other, more and more
beyond the camera's reach,
an intimation of endlessness lent to the child
who turned the page from August to September,
the month of her birth, the month of school and its rupture.

There would be no escaping the vast and hungry future.

3.
An Encounter with an Admired Person

This writing prompt is based on the teaching of Meg Pokrass (*Alligators at Night, The Dog Looks Happy Upsidedown*). In Pokrass's classes (usually for flash fiction or micro-memoir), she often presents inspiring contemporary models and surreal or whimsical vintage and archival photographs to help writers generate lively, original works. According to Pokrass, both poetry and flash fiction "come from injecting oneself (or one's characters) with a strong sense of emotional urgency."

Write a microfiction or poem in which you imagine an encounter with an admired person, someone who has had an influence on you and your work. As preparation, read Meg Pokrass's microfiction "My Imaginary Takeout with Lydia Davis." Communicate emotional urgency through language, imagery, and tone. An added challenge: try to incorporate into your writing five words from Pokrass's story, or from one of the other stories in this chapter.

Meg Pokrass

MY IMAGINARY CHINESE TAKEOUT WITH LYDIA DAVIS

A strange smell is coming from Lydia Davis's dog, our Chinese-take-out food, or me. Lydia is talking very brilliantly about her former mother-in-law and not making sense in a very lovely way. I could listen to her not making sense for hours.

I'm guessing she does not smell what I am smelling as her face seems calm. I hope she will continue talking about relatives to take my mind off the sulfurous air issue. It is probably coming from her dog. But it would be rude to assume anything, to say anything at all.

I can taste banana in my mouth though I have not had a banana in years and we are not eating bananas.

When we finish eating, it gets very quiet, and she sighs. Her dog sighs too. Then I sigh. We are an orchestra. And the smell seems gone.

I suggest we open our fortune cookies and Lydia agrees. As soon as she opens hers, and doesn't read what it says to me, I excuse myself. I am suddenly shy about what mine might say. She would not tell me what hers said, which may be why I got shy about mine.

In Lydia Davis's bathroom I am sitting on her toilet, unable to pee. I imagine my fingers dangling in a bowl of warm water. My muscles are tense and nothing is going to make it come out.

From the safe perch of her toilet, I memorize the names of her personal-care products, which are lined up on her bathroom shelf, watching. Lydia's personal-care products have the same names as the ones I use, which is strange, because I am broke.

There are so many things not to say to her when I return. I hope the smell is still gone. I hope I can figure out what not to say.

Valerie Fox

HEY THERE HARUKI, SORRY TO INTERRUPT YOUR RUN

I was an extra in that passage with Betty (Akiko) and the guy with the sheepish grin. I was eating a hot dog in Doutor by Yotsuya JR station near where I was working. I had a sweet gig teaching English to salarymen. My boyfriend was a civil servant, something to do with tin cans and jazz-whispering. So we've basically already met, I mean in your book.

In this other book of yours I was a snake-dog in an old man's pocket. I don't know how you knew where to find me to put me in that pocket but since it was before the Internet I am a little surprised you managed to find my shocked expression and quivering eyelids.

I took a panoramic picture of some giant crows and antennae and rooftops outside my balcony on my last day in Tokyo. A couple of years later I tried to paint a picture of this one specific crow. She was the one who'd been spotted arranging stones on the train tracks, on a whim, just to see what would happen. She told me all about it, out on the balcony. She made it onto the nightly news. I remember jumping up and down, I kept shouting, *I know that crow, I know that crow.*

Hey, I'm really into vinyl, just like you, Murakami-san. Do you want to come over to my small apartment and spin a few discs? Shit, I can't keep up. I'm glad this is New York City otherwise someone might call the cops and get me into some trouble, haha. I guess this looks a little strange. Everything I know about Beethoven I started to learn from you. Hey, wait, please, I'd sure like to pick your brain about your favorite recordings of Eureka, hey, that's okay, yes, I am busy too. It's hard to run away and talk at the same time.

Alicia Askenase

BRUSH WITH YOKO ONO

Yoko,

I caught sight of you last week near the Museum of Modern Art. I cannot believe you are 85 years old. I am thirteen, also getting up there. As a male I've always thought you a beautiful woman, with a unique birdlike voice:

1. inside and out, and,
2. *you can be wild and still be very wise* (your words)

I'm the cardinal that was in the honey locust to the right of the entrance. I heard you speaking with Sean as you stood outside, and I sang a tune, so if you heard, "cheeeer-a-dote, cheeer-a-dote-dote-dote," or "purdy, purdy, purdy...whoit, whoit, whoit, whoit," that was me.

I've always been considered a bit wild, or so I see myself, and the other cardinals would tease and say I was too assertive, too brave. For me, you are beyond brave, a maverick, an artist ahead of her time. Like you, my art is song, though I know you work in other genres.

My grandmother once lived in an ash near the Dakota, and sang highly of you and John, which is why, I admit, I followed you to the MOMA. She could sense both of you were special in some way from the vibrations that surrounded you. She sang to you as well. Our melody has been passed down for many generations, as far back as the dinosaurs.

Your and John's music would be playing in apartments and from open windows throughout the city when I first noted it. It made me stop dead in my flight. Because I understand some human sounds in English, I have peeked at your books in store windows, too. *Grapefruit*. What a strange title! But I like it.

I must be flying, but I want to tell you again how much I admire you, and how deeply sad I was when John was taken from you… Please tell Sean I say hello.

He seems very cool from the times I have seen him about. You raised him well alone. I hope we meet up soon… if you think you hear me, look up. I'll give you a nod with my beak; sing a little louder, for you, dear Yoko.

4.
Swipe a Line, Find a Title

A number of well-known poets have swiped lines from other poets' poems to create powerful titles. Robert Lowell and A. E. Stallings each have poems entitled (with slightly different spellings) "To Speke of Wo That Is in Mariage," a line from the Prologue to the Wife of Bath's Tale from Chaucer's *Canterbury Tales*. Lowell's and Stallings' poems depict contemporary women caught in marital strife.

This chapter draws specifically on the work of Christopher Bursk, who uses lines from Shakespeare's sonnets as the titles of the poems in his collection *The Infatuations and Infidelities of Pronouns*. Bursk sometimes reverses the theme or mood of the triggering poem. In this chapter, we include two examples by Bursk as well as an example by Jacquiley Wong. In "We Forget the Things We Didn't Say," Wong continues the tone set by A.E. Stallings' triggering poem, "On Visiting a Borrowed Country House in Arcadia."

For your swipe-a-line poem, take a provocative, mysterious, or otherwise powerful line from another poet's poem and make it the title of your poem. Then, respond to that title line in your poem. Your poem might depart radically from the originating poem's mood or message. Alternatively, your poem could also be an homage to or an updated version of some aspect of the originating poem.

You can pull your titles from poems from the tradition or contemporary poems. While your reader may not recognize your title line, he or she may have a hunch that the line is an allusion and might do a little research to track down the originating text. To signal that you are alluding to another work, consider a special type treatment for your title. For example, you might italicize your borrowed title line or enclose it in quotes. If the title line is not easily recognizable as a line from a well-known poem, add an epigraph that

mentions the name of the original poet or quote a few lines from the triggering poem along with the poet's name.

The lines Bursk uses come from any one of the original sonnet's
fourteen lines. In the example below, Bursk makes the last line from Shakespeare's Sonnet 50 the title for his poem, and he reverses the mood. Shakespeare's poem is all about slowness and moving away; Bursk's is about speed
and collision. Here's Bursk's poem:

MY GRIEF LIES ONWARD, AND MY JOY BEHIND
from Shakespeare's Sonnet 50

Afterwards, I was still stomping on the brake,
the car still hurling ahead as if it couldn't wait
to smash into the car in front, the hood still crumpling,
the windshield glass leaping with glee
at being set free, the present colliding with the future
and the future refusing to give, and then it was the past and it reeked
of anti-freeze. I'd almost killed someone. *Almost.*
No Shakespearean tragedy. Just an accident
though there was plenty of drama, the mind imagining
what might've happened till it *almost* seemed
it had, the subjunctive lifting its gun and fixing me in its sights.
Desire. Did all the circles in Hell circle back to it?
No, Hell was what might've been. It was Time
driving off. I could still see its taillights.

Here's the text of the originating Shakespeare poem:

SONNET 50

How heavy do I journey on the way,
When what I seek, my weary travel's end,
Doth teach that ease and that repose to say,
'Thus far the miles are measured from thy friend!'
The beast that bears me, tired with my woe,
Plods dully on, to bear that weight in me,
As if by some instinct the wretch did know
His rider loved not speed, being made from thee:

The bloody spur cannot provoke him on
That sometimes anger thrusts into his hide;
Which heavily he answers with a groan,
More sharp to me than spurring to his side;
 For that same groan doth put this in my mind;
 My grief lies onward, and my joy behind.

Here's a second example from Bursk's collection:

YOU ARE SO STRONGLY IN MY PURPOSE BRED
 from Shakespeare's Sonnet 112

I couldn't imagine a world without *you* and *me*,
even though those two pronouns often ended up like us
in a clash of wills; at the drive-in, *you* undressing *me*
as if I were a professional virgin like Doris Day,
and my father's Chrysler would do for a marriage bed.
You tried to get *me* so aroused I'd forget the cars
on either side. How could I expect to lose my virginity
with a 40-foot Rock Hudson looming over our heads?
As each soldier died gallantly on the screen,
I was supposed to take Iwo Jima and plant my flag?
I kept hoping one of those movie stars might take pity
and climb off the screen and help *me* engineer
my retreat from *you*. I could've used another set of
hands, another more knowledgeable pronoun in *our* backseat.

Jacquiley Wong

WE FORGET THE THINGS WE DIDN'T SAY
from A.E. Stallings' "On Visiting a Borrowed Country House in Arcadia"

Sometimes I lie awake in bed
And stare into the dark abyss,
Eyes wide, remembering all I said
When we were on the precipice.

Those words like sour milk I spat
In hasty anger, unrestrained—
You soaked them up then threw them back,
And on my mind left them ingrained.

I wonder, in my sleepless state,
What could have been, if I'd been honest.
But we forget the things we didn't say
And everything we never promised.

5.
Chances Are (You May Write a Great Poem Today): The Song-Title Prompt

This chapter fits into a theme we develop elsewhere in this book, using found language, and also, investigating the non-literary art forms or disciplines to find inspiration. Song titles are often fanciful, heartfelt, catchy, clever, mysterious: poetic, in short. Weaving them into a poem may help you blend art forms or develop an idea in a completely unexpected way. (Do take note that while using song titles is acceptable, quoting song lyrics without gaining the proper permissions is against fair use practice.)

This prompt is procedural and involves a couple of steps, in the sense that it may involve your finding and combining the words of others. If you write centos, which involve collaging lines from other writers' poems, you may find a similar feeling in your writing here, depending on how you interpret the prompt.

Here are some guidelines to help get you started. Make a list of song titles from an album. For instance, here are the titles from Johnny Mathis's album *Johnny's Greatest Hits* (Columbia, 1958).

Chances are
All the time
The twelfth of never
When sunny gets blue
When I am with you
Wonderful! Wonderful!
It's not for me to say
Come to me
Wild is the wind
Warm and tender
No love
I look at you

Use the titles as the spine or structure for the poem. If you have a CD or vinyl, the album cover imagery may also help you to generate your poem.

Next, create a rule or two, such as the following, and write a first draft. Here are a few suggested rules or constraints.

Use all of the titles, or as many as possible.

Write them out with space between, with the intention of filling in your own words between the titles.

Add a specified number of words or syllables to lines or sentences based on titles.

If the words are cliché, strive to use them anyway, to defamiliarize them, somehow.

For the next draft, you will have to decide how much you will want to edit. But for that first draft, try to stick with your original rules. Your rules need not be evident to readers.

Astute readers will notice patterns you create, or connections to the source music. Rina Terry's "Pearl Before Swine" becomes more poignant, perhaps, if you know Janis Joplin's songs deeply. But even if not, as a writer (someone who probably likes to "look under the hood," so to speak), you will notice how Terry's narrator's identification and homage to Janis's work gives a bluesy inflection to her own journey.

Rina Terry relies on titles from Joplin's *Pearl*. Benjamin Teperov's poem relies on song titles from Utada Ikaru's album *Fantôme*. Bernadette McBride takes song titles from Cat Stevens' *Tea for the Tillerman*. Joanne Leva uses Carole King's *Tapestry* as a resource. For her poem, Briyanna Hymms draws on the Day6 album *Moonrise*.

Rina Terry

PEARL BEFORE SWINE

That ball and chain of responsibility had kept me in place
even when I dreamed of a move over the fixed boundaries
of seven states. I can still hear the sea battle a nor'easter.

I have been farther west than this and said, "Bye, Bye, Baby"
time after time, move after move—no wonder changing
geography is the only way I can find a place to curse home.

An adventure, I called it at the time. Get it while you can,
I thought, but some were down on me for finally escaping
and I blasted "Me and Bobby McGee" all the way cross country.

I'm no cry baby but I still grieve the loss of that first house
in the field even though any city would be a better place now
that living alone means I have to try just a little bit harder.

It's summertime here in the mountains, still green, because
snow fell throughout spring and the thaw filled the streams,
rivers, reservoirs and a small drowning piece of my heart.

Benjamin Teperov

FANTÓME

Sometimes I stop, peering down the road and trying to make out shapes
    in the fog
There is something hanging from the trees. Yellow eyes wide. Watching—
—"What are you?" I call out.
It grins wider, mocking me in my own voice
"*Ore no kanojo?*" I echo, "Maybe I should bring a bouquet for you."

I looked away, into the trees and the mist. If I went off the path for a
    little bit—
just a two-hour vacation—
what would I see there?
A mermaid, twisting through the grey air,
or jewelweeds twined together with their friends?
I could catch a midsummer shower,
run with the wolves in the wilderness,
follow them to the edge of the trees and peer into oblivion—
It might be the best day of my life.

I step forward onto the road, flowing cherry blossoms catching in my hair.

Bernadette McBride

BUT I MIGHT DIE TONIGHT
—Small-time Country Singer Shadows
Cat's *Tea for the Tillerman* Plus One

At fifteen, a huddled moonshadow
on her bedroom wall each night, Sad Lisa
wondered where do the children play?
She could sing, write, play danged well.

But who cared? Grown up in Nowhere,
small town that finally chased her out
at sixteen by pea brains and cheap talk—
rucksack on her back, guitar case at her feet,

she hitched a ride West with a hippie
father and son who picked her up
along their way, too, on the road to find out.
Two days later they dropped her in Austin

where she holed up in flop houses,
picked up gigs in dives, made herself
a local name. Pretty soon she scored
some regular notice in the town papers,

booked more bars across eight states
than she could count, even cut a record
that made it to some radio stations down South.
She met a lot of cowboys who followed her

like hungry puppies—married three of them
over thirteen years. Kept her maiden name
long before it was okay, knowing,
hard-headed woman she was, some day

she'd find longer boats to board, head out
of her wild world. When someday came,
she knew—high-tailed into white horizons,
settled on a big-sky ranch with a fine porch

for guitar-pickin', finally able to exhale long,
stand alone in the wind, arms parallel
to the blowing switchgrass. Miles and miles
…and miles from Nowhere.

Joanne Leva

ENDURING ODE
—for my daughter

It's too late for Smackwater Jack, the giant garbage heap from which our
    lives rose out of like polluting steam.
But beautiful daughter,
I will follow where you lead, (in the symbolic sense)
aging and decrepit, yet thriving!

Well in the game of interpreting tomorrows, horrors, and terrors, I'll refrain
from simple single-mindedness. Instead I'll hover
like a foraging bird, over a blank page,
abundant and restored.

In an instant, I feel the earth move
and the doors of involuntary recollection open in one lightning flash
and we're home again.
Way over yonder in our first apartment

after 5 years with my parents, after the divorce.
We were glued to the ceiling, celebrating periodic deaths and rebirths
of exorcised demons.
What an extraordinary rhapsody that seems so far away now.

It's like our own little dysfunctional tapestry, that we are shackled to and
    free from your bitter joke of a father.
So when time attempts to end a story that can never be ended,
always remember you've got a friend and you make me feel (seriously)
like a natural woman.

But will you love me tomorrow?

Briyanna Hymms

DAY6 - *MOONRISE*

1. Better Better,
        i liked you best;
        have you come up with an excuse for me?
2. I Like You
        though i think we keep dancing
        in circles
3. What Can I Do
        except stay in my routine?
        i'm not going to break my own comfort for you
4. I'll Remember
        all the missed moments,
        all the stolen stares
5. Whatever!
        stop this, you're leaving soon!
        he gave no hints anyways
6. Be Lazy
        be cautious, be careless, be myself
        maybe the cycle will never break
7. Hi Hello
        yes, it started this way
        you never asked me my name then
8. I Loved You
        but perhaps it's the same way i loved
        everyone who came into my heart
9. When You Love Someone
        doesn't it show in your eyes?
        i thought everyone could read mine
10. All Alone
        in this sterile room
        i have so much space to think
11. Pouring
        out all my thoughts onto graph paper
        i'm trying to reach a conclusion

12. I Need Somebody
> i needed a body
> it would be unfair if i "loved" you

13. I'll Try
> to stop myself from going farther
> beyond just physical affection

6.
The Thank-You Poem

Reach deep within yourself to write a poem of gratitude to a parent, a friend or stranger who was there for you in your time of need, a loyal pet, a car that got you where you needed to go, a season you love, or any other person, place, thing, or idea to which you are grateful. From the biblical psalms of thanksgiving to the most modern expressions of personal gratitude, the poem of thanks allows you to express and expand your feelings of appreciation, even when those feelings might be too late in coming, such as Robert Hayden's gratitude to his father in his much-anthologized classic "Those Winter Sundays." A poem of gratitude can be deeply spiritual. It might even be peppery, painful, and ironic depending on the situation and who is being thanked.

Paul Laurence Dunbar

A THANKSGIVING POEM

The sun hath shed its kindly light,
  Our harvesting is gladly o'er
Our fields have felt no killing blight,
  Our bins are filled with goodly store.

From pestilence, fire, flood, and sword
  We have been spared by thy decree,
And now with humble hearts, O Lord,
  We come to pay our thanks to thee.

We feel that had our merits been
  The measure of thy gifts to us,
We erring children, born of sin,
  Might not now be rejoicing thus.

No deed of ours hath brought us grace;
  When thou were nigh our sight was dull,
We hid in trembling from thy face,
  But thou, O God, wert merciful.

Thy mighty hand o'er all the land
  Hath still been open to bestow
Those blessings which our wants demand
  From heaven, whence all blessings flow.

Thou hast, with ever watchful eye,
  Looked down on us with holy care,
And from thy storehouse in the sky
  Hast scattered plenty everywhere.

Then lift we up our songs of praise
  To thee, O Father, good and kind;
To thee we consecrate our days;
  Be thine the temple of each mind.

With incense sweet our thanks ascend;
　Before thy works our powers pall;
Though we should strive years without end,
　We could not thank thee for them all.

Amir Or

6: THANKS FOR THE EVENING SKY

Thanks for the evening sky, thanks for clouds,
food courts, billboards, trashcans, benches.
Thanks for trees, for the anxious morning light,
for the life that trickles through my limbs,
for motion and rest,
for the words to say
thanks

Amberlyn Wilk

A LETTER TO MY RAPIST

Thank you.
Because of you trying to rip out every ounce of strength
I had in my small teenage body,
I discovered all of the strength I really do have.
An inner strength that you and your
evil actions could never take away from me.

Thank you.
Because when you ripped away all of my childhood
and drained the last drops of innocence
running through my veins
I grew up that day.
I grew up and toughened up
and learned that nothing in the world
could ever break me.

Thank you
for filling me with so much sadness and shame
that I swore I was about to drown.
Thank you for that
because I learned that there were people around me
who were willing to jump in and help me to shore.
And I learned that those who didn't
were better left drifting away.

With this letter to you,
I just want you to understand that
you didn't break me.
I have thrown off the blanket of shame
you tried to smother me with.
I'm free.

Katrina Wehr

A THANK-YOU NOTE FOR MEGAN

After he left
I slammed the door
turned the lock
slid the chain
sat on the floor

It doesn't look like it now
but I'm glad he's gone
He was never any good for me anyway
Lying, pushing, arguing
manipulating

First it was Ariel
followed by Kirsten, or Kristen
You can't expect me to keep them all straight
Then there was a Lauren
and finally a Megan

He had a perfectly practiced answer
to every question asked
And a strong arm
to keep a girlfriend in her place
at the bottom of his list

Ariel should have been a warning sign
Kirsten (or Kristen) a red flag
Lauren should have been strike three
But Megan finally tipped the scale
I guess I should thank her

My brain took the wheel from my heart
I stopped wearing rose-colored glasses
put out the burning torch

and took back the keys
Time to close this door forever

Burn the photos
Raise the standards higher
Skip this chapter
Lay down more brick on the wall
Add a new lock on the door

7.
The I-Hate Poem

The I-hate poem can be a rant about things in general or it can be a screed against a specific person or event. Invective can be very inspiring and satisfying, and the I-hate poem lets you express on the page all the things you can't say to your antagonist's face. It frees you to list his or her crimes both major and minor. The I-hate poem is not just therapy; it is also art, and because of that it should include a range of emotional tones and evocative images. The I-hate poem tends to be fierce and fast paced. Depending on how over-the-top you allow your invective to be, the I-hate poem might even include some self-indictment or allusions to your own weakness or fears. On the other hand, the literary speaker need not be you. You might write an I-hate poem through a persona.

Diane Lockward

INVECTIVE AGAINST THE BUMBLEBEE

Escapee from a tight cell, yellow-streaked,
sex-deprived sycophant to a queen,
you have dug divots in my yard
and like a squatter trespassed in my garage.

I despise you for you have swooped down
on my baby boy, harmless on a blanket of lawn,
his belly plumping through his orange stretch suit,
yellow hat over the fuzz of his head.
Though you mistook him for a sunflower,
I do not exonerate you,
for he weeps in my arms, trembles, and drools,
finger swollen like a breakfast sausage.
Now my son knows pain.
Now he fears the grass.

Fat-assed insect! Perverse pedagogue!
Henceforth, may flowers refuse to open for you.
May cats chase you in the garden.
I want you shellacked by rain, pecked by shrikes,
mauled by skunks, paralyzed by early frost.
May farmers douse your wings with pesticide.
May you never again taste the nectar
of purple clover or honeysuckle.
May you pass by an oak tree just in time
to be pissed on by a dog.

And tomorrow may you rest on my table
as I peruse the paper. May you shake
beneath the scarred face of a serial killer.

Kevin Hughes

I CAN'T STAND YOU

I can't stand you like I can't stand a paper cut,
Like I can't stand that guy
Talking on his cell phone in the library,
Like I can't stand driving behind a grandmother.

I can't stand you any more than I can stand
A smudge on my glasses,
Or a bug on my windshield,
Or a pimple on my nose.

I can't stand you the way
Poets can't stand clichés,
Nuns sacrilege,
Or teachers teacher's pets.

I hate the way you can't take a joke—Erin McCourt

Erin McCourt

YOU

I hate your hat. The blue one, that's faded.
I hate that you wear it to cover thinning hair.
Just own it.
I hate the way you can't take a joke
and don't vote.
I hate how you only drink craft beers
and judge all those holding a Miller Lite.
I hate the way you text. Perfect punctuation and caps
yet a short U,
a number 4,
T.H.X.

I hate that you think bartenders
are your real friends.
I hate your love of anime, *Star Wars*, how you never have bus
tokens, that you won't join Facebook,
your ugly cat, your too-big Yale jacket,
but, what
I despise
is that it doesn't matter to you anymore, anyway.

8.
Change a Moment in Time

The idea visits us in troubling times or happy times: how might life have been different if one had taken or not taken a certain action, said or not said something, met or not met a specific person, not showed up at the wrong place at the wrong time?

This prompt, called change a moment in time, asks you to explore how life might have been otherwise.

Here's one approach: Write a poem that reflects on this idea: If you could replace a moment in time, what moment would you choose to replace? And if you did transform that moment, how might life have been altered?

You might prefer to engage the idea with a two-step approach. Start with an if/then formula, such as one of these:

If my wallet had not been stolen...

If I'd apologized to my friend for not inviting her to the party/sharing her secret/or other troubling thing...

If Eve had told Satan to bug off...

If Jerry had not introduced us...

Write for 10 minutes.

Now write a second part to your poem in which you incorporate any or all of the following: a phrase from the part you have already written, a new fictional character or real person, a personal or philosophical reflection, a parallel or contrasting event.

Write for 10 minutes.

And, then, of course, revise.

Grant Clauser

FOLLOWING RIVERS

I should have said yes, should have stayed
for one more day, watched the sunrise turn
even the tar paper rooftops into something golden,
how rain over the milltown makes all the edges
soft, like a hillside worn down from seasons
becomes a home you can imagine building.

So when I watched you shrink behind
the closing door, each step farther away
chipped the edges from that image, no
home, no sunrise starting at the mountain
and gliding across the river to our porch,
no hillside, but the mill falling into decay.

So years later, when I did finally have the strength
to say yes, another river flowing below another
bridge, another woman closing a door, this time
both of us settled behind it, I couldn't help
but think of you, the way you said I'd always
follow a river home, no matter where it ended.

Jerry Mirskin

MIKE

In New York freezing is about forty-two inches.
That's how far you have to dig if you're putting in a foundation.
In this case, we were digging by hand because the backhoe couldn't get in.
I'd done work like that before. One time on a farm, I had to dig
a grave for a calf. I remember I was up to my waist in the hole.
It was winter, the farmer came by, looked down
and said, That's deep enough.
Another time, I was digging and found a row of horse teeth.
They were coated with dirt, but after I cleaned them off, I realized
that they weren't teeth, but a row of keys from an adding machine.
I remember holding the unearthed numbers in my hand.
They'd been in the ground for some time, but I had a feeling
they could still add.

Now it was summer and hot. Over ninety degrees.
The foreman came by. Mike. He was a good guy, but I couldn't see it.
All the others were inside, and I was out there in the heat.
He picked up a shovel.
It wasn't work that a master carpenter would do but he started in.
I wasn't assuaged. I wanted to know why I was the one in the hole.
He didn't say.
I knew a little bit about him. He had graduated high school
and went right to work. By the time he was twenty-five
he was an accomplished craftsman and even taught a class in construction
at the local community college. I also knew that he was recently married.
His wife, a cute but tough girl, drove motorcycles in a circus.
She was one of the riders in the round steel cage, going around and around
and upside down, held by centrifugal force.
Often there was more than one motorcycle in there.
It was really loud and smoky, and you wondered how they didn't get dizzy
or collide and crash.

Mike was in love with her. The circus was in Florida.
One night she called him. They had been going together on and off.
She was sick of it, but didn't know what to do.
Mike got into his car that night and drove twenty hours to where she was.
He proposed and they came back together.
He would talk about her.
Sometimes he would even share some of the private things they did.
Other times he talked about how he'd come home from work, tired.
She wasn't working and she was lonely and wanted to play.
He told me how he used to stop at a park on the way home sometimes
and take a nap, so that he had energy to be with her.
I pictured him lying on the grass in some park.
Resting between his work life and his home life.
We were digging. After a while, we stopped to take a drink.
The sweat was pouring off. He looked at me.
I realized that he'd probably have to go back inside, but he didn't go in.
Instead he started talking. He said that his dad died five years ago.
He said that he couldn't get used to the idea that he would never
see him again. His dad would never see him with a good job and a wife
and all they were planning.
I hadn't ever seen him upset.
I haven't actually seen a lot of men upset.
He said he would work for a whole year in a trench and give all his pay
if he could just see his dad for five minutes.
A year of one's life for five minutes.
I tried to picture that meeting. The meeting that couldn't happen.
The truth was as flat and hot as the face of a shovel.
For a moment there was quiet. There was sadness, but it felt peaceful.
After a while, Mike went back into the house, and I went back to digging.
Back to the girl in the cage. Back to driving all night long on the highway.

Amberlyn Wilk

BLACK AND BLUE

It all started when you traded in your blond locks for blue.
You went from a potato to 80-proof vodka.
Maybe that was the day I should have begun to distance myself from you,
but I didn't know about the life you planned
when you stepped out of the Dye Hard Salon with your dirty black
      Converses.

Your dirty black Converses,

the ones that you wore when you bought heroin for the first time
at the run-down playground on 39th Street.
Your mom called my mom, crying about where she went wrong.
Maybe if you hadn't been so concerned
with wearing your rebellious spirit like a badge of honor
you wouldn't be in jail now, wasting away.

9.
Bibliomancy

Bibliomancy was a kind of divination based on the consultation of books, especially the Bible, or Homer's works. The practice involved locating passages, at random, for interpretation.

This prompt asks you to draw on quotations from books to help you create a poem. Anything goes, but works that compile aphorisms, lore, and famous quotations are good places to start. Even if your selection is based seemingly on chance, perhaps on some books you have scattered around your study, your mind will work both analytically and intuitively to connect passages, words, ideas.

Here's a way to start. Make a list of quotations that you find engaging or memorable. Use the quotations as the spine or basis for your poem.

Attribution of your sources is often a part of how you will present your finished work. In terms of attribution, a brief note on process will interest your readers. If you aren't sure about how or whether to mention sources, take the time to explore fair use practices to make sure that you are being ethical in how you present your writing.

Here, in their own words, are the ways that our contributors have used bibliomancy to create poems:

Luray Gross, on *"Dolce Far Niente"*: For finding aphorisms I browsed through a 1980 version of *Bartlett's Familiar Quotations*. I incorporated Horace, Mark Twain, E.B. White, and a comment made by Xavier Le Pichon during a radio interview. The latter remark provided the necessary tension to bring the poem to life.

Leonard Gontarek, on "Nest": I bought this *Compton's Pictured Encyclopedia and Fact-Index*, 1940, in a used bookstore. It was the surviving volume of a set. Its attraction was its maps, diagrams and beautiful color plates. A very different encounter with information when compared to online searches. I began typing out the ones on the section on birds to have a closer look. This was the process. How the poem came about is harder to describe. Perhaps the book's being from the past unloosened the personal and family history and its connection to nests. Clearly, the poem was drawn from the material. I permit my poetry to be available to any source it wishes.

Christine Hamm: Luckily, while writing "At Ghost Falls," I was working on my doctoral dissertation chapter on poet Marianne Moore, who kept boxes and boxes of notebooks wherein she wrote down many thousands of lines, phrases, utterances, headlines from museum placards, and other scraps of text so that she could later collage them into poems. I started to do something similar, going through various memoirs, biographies, science texts, and other books, noting lines that caught my fancy. This exercise helped me to stretch myself, to adopt metaphors and language that I wouldn't otherwise have used. Specifically, I modify pieces found in Berryman's Dream Songs. I also incorporate phrases in two lines from *A Closer Look at Ariel: A Memory of Sylvia Plath* by Nancy Hunter Steiner.

Devin Williams: While browsing the reference section of the library, I came across *The Encyclopedia of Animal Symbolism in Art* by Hope B. Werness. I immediately turned to the page about one of my favorite animals, rats. I was intrigued by the fact that rats represented so many different things in cultures around the world. I knew I wanted to write a poem celebrating this often unappreciated and hated species for their intelligence and sentience. So, I picked out the most empowering words and phrases from the book, and combined them with my own knowledge about rats, as well as facts I found in *Wildlife of the Mid-Atlantic* by John H. Rappole.

Your way of using this prompt may be to read slowly and deeply. It may be a way to deal with the inundation of information we sometimes feel subjected to, or purposefully engage with. If you want to energize your writing, if you are in a bit of a rut, using research in this way may help you create a draft or template. You may well feel a fun sense of doing collage and physical activity, as well. Your early draft might be kind of messy—don't worry about that. If that's the case, use that draft as an outline, as a way to collect your thoughts.

For a look at conceptual (found) work, check out the work of Robert Fitterman, including "A Hemingway Reader: *The Sun Also Rises*." Earlier precursors include Jackson Mac Low's *The Virginia Woolf Poems* and David Antin's *Code of Flag Behavior*.

Just me in the café, in the afternoon—Leonard Gontarek

Luray Gross

DOLCE FAR NIENTE

Among my prayers, a long day
of sweet doing-nothing
with my heart skilled
in the works of both languages—
that of touch
and that of silence,
submitting nothing
to the tribe I have left behind.

A day when weather
is my only literary speciality
and nothing discourages, not even
the pecking of a neighbor's chickens
spearing bugs among the weeds
in the kingdom of their portable yard.

It will be morning as long as I prefer
and afternoon far beyond the slanted light.
How sweet it will be to let the mind unbend,
easy as stretching out a coil of shoelace licorice,
simple as smoothing a hem
before taking up needle and thread.

The heart cannot be educated by itself,
I heard a wise man say.
Perhaps he was correct,
but I want to take my little soul
into a place never known for instruction
where wine tastes pure as water
and poems please and last.

Leonard Gontarek

NEST

1

Just me in the café, in the afternoon,
and a bunch of Ethiopians
and soft socialists and a
mother with two kids in a double stroller.
Light and its affiliates.

2

Hi, I'm Leonard, I've got like 30 dirty dishes in the sink,
and I think I was partially brain-damaged in the bus accident,
I can't do simple math, I don't remember things,

I'm a messy eater, I can't sew, and I stole this shirt.
And I hear a fax sound in my head.
I thought you'd appreciate my honesty.

You ever notice, they don't make mouse-flavored cat food.
Why don't they make mouse-flavored cat food?

Know how I get a seat to myself on the subway?
I say, *Excuse me, Jesus is sitting here.*
For either of those reasons I get the seat to myself.

Those stories about trapped people resorting to cannibalism, I believe it.
I never get on an elevator unless someone looks good enough to eat.

I'm the one who yelled Encore at the Who concert,
after they destroyed all their instruments.

If you laid all the stupid people in the world end to end around the equator,
well, they'd have to be to let you do that to them.

I hope all the stupid people in the world got that way
by fucking their brains out.

People seem confused by my My Other Poem Is A Sestina bumper sticker.
I used to be crazy, but now I see Sigmund Freud twice a week and I'm
   much better.

3

The drawings make the design clear.
The ceiling can be removed for cleaning out the house.
It should slope upward so rain will not run in.
Painting the house inside and out will make it last longer.

4

In the evergreen trees of Canada,
the gentle cedar waxwings build their nests.
The one shown here may be male or female,
for the two sexes look alike.

5

When my parents were hurried off by aliens,
there were lots of lights.

6

Our home was filled with compressed roses
and painted aluminum Eighties' abstracts.

7

Blue is blowing and snowing.
Sad frightened running.
Homes unloved and beautiful.
Slick barn cock wind clicks.

8

Homeless, faces ruddy as bankers,
workers circle and taunt them,
tell them their hunger is good.
My father calls out in his sleep.

9

The northern parula warbler
always makes its exquisite nest
of usnea moss.

10

The white-throated nuthatch (upper left)
prefers a hole in a forest tree.

11

Asterisks of seeds fly weightless from the tree
whose name was a mystery when we arrived here
and remains one.

12

Flying is what we are thinking about here.
Flying over and into the present.
Soft-focus, the Queen of the Birds drops like a barrel into pond
from rooftop.

13

The brilliant cardinal and his noisy, quarrelsome, but beautiful neighbor
seem to seek human companionship.

14

After the fall molt, the bobolink looks like a large sparrow.

15

The graceful barn swallow
builds its nest of mud and grasses.
A clump of weeds conceals
the beautifully arched nest

of the meadowlark.
These male birds help the females
feed their large families.

16

The pyrrhuloxia (above)
is a relative of the cardinal.
It nests in mesquite thickets.
The male has just brought food
to the brooding female.

17

When my parents were swept off by aliens,
there were lots and lots of lights.

18

When my grandparents stepped on the shore,
they could not make out the name of the ship.

Praise there was mist and the river was slate
and silver and unraveled. There was too much mist.

Praise the flowers which opened in the weeds.
They were iris. This is what my grandmother looked at.

Praise my grandfather's heart which was heavy,
it was twice its weight.

He knew this was the land in which his sons would die,
one of them young. He already missed the trees.

Although there would be trees here,
praise the snow and awful scents they would fill with.

But it would not be like their snow.
I cannot tell you anything more about that morning.

Mornings are dreams and are forgotten when you look out a window.
Praise the birds which did not eat the worms, that morning.

Christine Hamm

AT GHOST FALLS

Your children crowd close to me, tiny warm slick bodies, trying to touch the railing, trying to finger the water's white noise.

In their shop-lifted pocketbooks: A poster of the falls in winter. A pair of falls-colored mittens. Falls-flavored doggie treats. A mini-handgun. A sample of water from the falls in a sealed teacup.

Your thickest glasses masquerade as mist-colored eyes on the back of your head. *You were supposed to cry,* you tell me, *in the movies, they always cry.*

In the damp, your hair fused into a muddy abomination, your feet, sweet fish, on the threshold of the elevator shaft, you say to me, *write about the black-winged redbird.*

It's red-winged, red-winged, I whisper.

I promised to hold your hand—I broke that promise, and I'm sorry.

I write about the red-winged blackbird flying to your ear before disappearing into the engine's white noise.

I write on your back as you're kneeling for a photo.

I write in children's broken cursive, in ink made of dirt and falls.

I write as if I'm blind and you're deaf—shapes punched into paper, wet, chewed and colorless.

(*There's no such thing as colorless,* you tell me.)

I think you've heard the terrible news: even the abnormally scrubbed and powerful one, the Girl Scout, ignores us when we sing.

But here's all my blood in a teacup, vulgar, gluttonous.

Devin Williams

RATS

Nesting in abandoned burrows,
Coastal cliffs,
And caves.

I am present when food is abundant.
Companion of Daikoku,
Savior of Sesshu,
First sign of the zodiac.

I am the scavenger of the night,
Recycling human refuse.

I am ruler of the underland.
Symbol of success
And prosperity,
Industry, and intelligence.

A prisoner of science,
I give you self-knowledge
And awareness.

I listen
With my nearly-naked ears.
I learn
From watching and repeating.
I feel
With my body *and* my soul.

It is only language that separates us.
Yet, you avoid
And attack me.
You don't *know* me,
How can you claim to know how I feel?

10.
The Cameo Cinquain

The cinquain is a five-line syllabic poem invented in the twentieth century by the American poet Adelaide Crapsey. Each line of the cinquain has a specific number of syllables; that is the only requirement of the form. Because the cinquain is so short and because brevity is the soul of wit, the cinquain's small stage lends itself to the poetic quip, the piquant observation, and especially to the cameo portrait. Consider capturing a unique aspect of a friend, enemy, co-worker, movie star, beloved pet, or anyone else whose personality you would like to frame in a poetic glimpse that concludes with a two-syllable snap.

Build your cameo cinquain around one signature characteristic of your subject: what habit, idiosyncrasy, or typical behavior is she famous for? What does he obsess about? Try to be a little loving or sympathetic most of the time. Skewer only when necessary. You may include the person's name (actual or made up) and some of his backstory or her typical turn of phrase or fashion statement. You might observe something about the person's fate. Because you only have twenty-two syllables to work with, you have to focus on compression.

The cinquain's five lines break down like this:

2 syllables
4 syllables
6 syllables
8 syllables
2 syllables

These are sound-syllables, not dictionary-divided syllables. The lines of a cinquain do not rhyme. Meter is optional: some poets say that the cinquain should be written in iambic feet, but this is not necessary. The lines need not be end-stopped. In fact, enjambing the lines, that is, allowing one line to flow to the next one without a comma or period, adds to the speed and freedom of this form.

From a pedagogical point of view, the cinquain offers a fun and no-stress introduction to syllabic poetry. The cinquain can also be seen as a stanza form: you could write a poem comprising a chain of cinquains. You could try a double cinquain (see Dawn Manning's "The Widow's Cinquains" in this chapter). While one can write a cinquain about anything—a street scene, a memory, or a bouquet of flowers—the cameo cinquain, like a brooch with a profile, allows this short form to speak of something deeper and more human.

CLASSROOM IDEA: THE GET-TO-KNOW-YOU CINQUAIN

Teachers and workshop leaders can use the get-to-know-you cinquain, a lighter form of the cameo cinquain, as an introductory exercise on the first meeting of a poetry-writing class. Put the class members in pairs, and then tell them to interview and observe one another for material to put in the cinquain. For example, you might stipulate that each cinquain should reference the person's name, one article of clothing that he or she is wearing, his or her favorite food or beverage, or maybe a sport or other recreational activity the person enjoys. You can make up your own list of ingredients. Write, then share. This also makes a fun party game.

Lynn Levin

RUHLMAN

Ruhlman
was a mean horse,
hated jockeys, stomped on
them. Few weep over his grave at
Old Friends.

JANICE

You stuffed
your training bra
with tissues, read stacks of
bodice rippers. Never found Sir
Perfect.

SANDRA

I called
the dog to kill
the rabbit eating my
garden. Does this make me a bad
human?

Dawn Manning

THE WIDOW'S CINQUAINS

I slip
into the heat
of his body sloughed off
in suburban sheets, draw warmth through
coiled limbs

and keep
watch over darkened windowpanes
for the ghost of scratched glass
made visible
by rain.

Kelly McQuain

SUPERMAN

Death-rays
bounce off his pecs;
Luthor's plan gets foiled. Clark's
weakness? Not kryptonite—but love:
Lois.

Miriam N. Kotzin

THE SPEAKER

Looks right
down his nose at
us, then grins and winks. When
a woman faints, he asks for water.
Hero.

Josh Romley

BANANA

The best.
The banana.
It is so subtly sweet.
Souls seek such succulent fruit. Shit.
I slipped.

TO MY ROOMMATE

Aaron,
the dishes are
piling up in the sink.
I did them last time you lazy
butthead.

Mirna Norales

MY HAMSTER, JOAN

Hamster
named Joan was an
ass of a pet. She kicked
me when I tried to pet her hair.
She's dead.

Dear Bee Lady: Many ask but when you answer
I don't understand. —John Timpane

11.
The Advice Column Poem

A host of columnists have been offering life advice to anonymous, and usually desperate, readers for generations. These columnists are as varied as the mainstream and fondly remembered "Dear Abby" and "Ann Landers," the hip Carolyn Hax of "Tell Me about It," the no-holds-barred sex-and-relationship expert Dan Savage of "Savage Love," "Ask E. Jean," who delivers a heady mix of endearments and well-researched replies to the readers of *Elle*, and many more. These columnists don't just provide help for the perplexed and frantic; they also provide writers with premium-grade grist for the poetic mill.

The advice-column poem is a two-part poem. It works especially well as a prose poem. The first part is a letter from the troubled party explaining the predicament. The second part is the solution offered by the advice columnist. You should structure your poem like an actual newspaper or magazine advice column, complete with salutation and closing. The title of your poem might imitate the headline over a daily advice column, such as "Boyfriend Refuses to Eat Vegetables." Your writer may have kid problems, a cheating spouse, a rowdy neighbor, a nosy boss. Your advisor may have level-headed advice, no clue at all, go off on a tangent, or be as obscure as the Oracle of Delphi.

Lauren Hall

LOST WITHOUT FRANK

Dear Madame Rosa,

I don't know what to do. My husband (we'll call him Frank) has left me for another woman. And not just any other woman—he's left me for a woman who doesn't exist. Some people have mid-life crises; well, Frank had a mid-life break with reality. One morning we were drinking our coffee at the kitchen table, and he asked, cream or sugar? Stop joking, I laughed, it's too early for jokes, and besides, you know I take it black. I wasn't asking you, he said, I was asking Georgina. And he stared in the direction of the toaster oven like she was lounging there in her silk pajamas, nibbling a scone. At first I thought he'd swiped another one of my Vicodins, but as the weeks went by, Georgina started joining us for breakfast every morning, and then dinner, too. Trips to the grocery store became impossible without asking Georgina about her food allergies. Our vacation was put on hold because Georgina developed a fear of flying. Eventually, I had enough. Either Georgina goes, or I go, I told him. It never occurred to me that Frank might go, too. Please, Madame Rosa, will you consult your crystal ball?

Lost without Frank
Annapolis, MD

Dear Lost,

Madame Rosa does not think you are so very lost. When I look into your future, there is no Frank, there is no Georgina. They are but specks of dust, flies in the ointment. You say this Georgina never existed, and there Madame Rosa agrees, but who's to say that Frank wasn't just more of the same? Who's to say you didn't make him up one afternoon while you were sorting your sock drawer or scrubbing the toilet? Hush. Someday we will all face our folly. Look into your own crystal ball, and what do you see? Bone and ash, cream and sugar. A moment in your mouth, my dear, and then it's gone. Madame Rosa cannot help you until you are ready for help. So many people, they come to me with questions they have already answered. Frank never left you, you woke up one morning and forgot he was there. It happens. So what? Maybe tomorrow he will return. Maybe tomorrow you will show up in another woman's kitchen and drink coffee with her husband. Maybe tomorrow you will pass a shop window and see your reflection there, hovering like another Georgina. Who can say?

Until then, I remain,
Madame Rosa

Aimee LeBrie

LIFE OF THE CUBED
(Dedicated to a contestant on *Jeopardy* who incorrectly solved the puzzle)

Dear Matilda,

I write to you because I know you understand the artistic temperament and how difficult it is to function in the 9-to-5 world. Sometimes, when I'm in meetings at work, I have an overwhelming urge to stand up, pull my shirt up over my head, and run screaming from the room. This usually happens when we're on the second to third PowerPoint presentation, but the urge can be brought on even by certain phrases, such as, "low-hanging fruit," "drill down," or "it is what it is." When I start to feel this way, I look around the room to catch the eyes of the other people sitting at the conference table, but no one seems to find anything wrong with the situation. They nod or add their own suggestions to "crunch the numbers" by "EOD" to check on the "ROI." Am I alone in feeling that we're wasting our lives on these meaningless things? Should I just accept the quote unquote status quo? Or should I chuck it all and go to graduate school to follow my dream of writing the great American novel? Please advise quickly; we have a two-day retreat coming up at the Sheraton Conference Center and I'm not sure I can stand another Meyers Briggs analysis (I always come out as INFJ).

Signed,
Stuck in a Cubicle with Nowhere to Turn

Dear Stuck,

We call this life. Get used to board/bored meetings. And more bad news—graduate school will have its own set of water-in-the-ear, irritating words and endless classes that test your ability to sit still and behave. You will find yourself listening to PhD students whose teeth seem stuck together when they speak of Nietzsche and Derrida as they argue the meaning of those very words in the sentences you mentioned. Your head will begin to feel heavy, as if filled with sand. You'll sleep with the wrong people (poets) and wake up hungover and late for the 8 AM Rhetoric and Composition class you must teach to bewildered freshmen who begin papers with sentences like "Since the beginning of time, mankind has loved Downy fabric softener…" You will try to write the great American novel and find that you only have one narrow story to tell; the one about not fitting in and, my darling, that has already been done to death.

My advice: accept your fate, get your paycheck, be nice to others, and above all, don't take your shirt off in a meeting unless it's being held in strip club in Vegas. At the same time, you must also pay attention, take notes, ask questions and consider alternate scenarios and then: go home to your tiny little studio apartment and write about it. Spill it all and be as mean and critical of yourself as you are to others. In that way, you might start to feel like a real person. In that way, you might become a writer. But you will never escape the feeling that you are alone, because you are. Just like the rest of us.

John Timpane

DEAR BEE LADY

Dear Bee Lady: Many ask but when you answer I don't understand. Problem: Happy marriage. Wealthy girl, good soldier, royal line. We lived the country life. I know, I know, everybody takes up shepherding. As if they think it changes anything. I know, I know, you can't run away by buying one hundred fleecy ruminants and chasing them around a moor with a dog. What else to do? My mother is Head Goddess and hates me. Here's how I know: One day I wake to find I gutted my sons and wife and slopped our home altar with their guts. Household and family tree polluted backward and forward through time. Solution?

Perplexed in Thebes

Dear Perp: Bee Lady here. Here's the Bee Line. What solves does not know what is solved. Change your name. You are now Hercules. See your cousin the king. He'll make you kill a lion and a Hydra (that won't count), capture a deer and a boar, clean out some guy's stables (that won't count), kill some birds, capture a bull, swipe some man-eating horses (he'll let them go), filch a queen's girdle (he'll keep it in his bedroom to smell), traverse the earth to steal some steer (he'll sacrifice them), steal some apples, and capture a three-headed dog. When you're done, no more monsters or magic, just people on a planet that scares them less. Retire with a new wife, who'll make you a tunic that burns you to death.

Have fun.

Bee Lady at the Bee Line

12.
The Faux Translation

Choose a poem to use as a source text in a language you don't know. You might choose one at random or one that appeals to you for a specific reason. Maybe you like the look of the poem, or maybe you can read it phonetically and appreciate how it sounds.

Write your "translation" based on the source text. You decide how much of the poem to use and how to "translate." You might try to use the entire poem, or you might not. You might rely on sound, sight, or both.

Some writers like to riff on a few words and ideas and come up with a poem wholly unlike the original. Some writers are taken with the idea of a faux translation as an invention or fiction. Imitation, parody, homage—writers have come up with a variety of tones and strategies. The faux translation can be a solo game, solitaire-style, or done with a group. It can help you get out of a rut, perhaps keep you from overthinking. For teachers, this is a terrific chance to write in class and work in groups.

Teachers, please share the examples and writers' processes in this book with your students. But we want to tell you that a spontaneous "jump right in" approach has also been very successful. Also, don't assume that you can't use a faux translation writing with young children or beginners. Young kids might warm up with a group writing.

Working poets may notice right away that faux translation activities resemble surrealistic games with their purported capacity to open up the subconscious. Writers report that this gives them a chance to use language imaginatively, and to explore some ideas or images through a new lens.

Some of the contributors here include notes on process, following their poems.

Marshall Warfield

LEAVING THE PALEOLITHIC

Lay the blanket here on cool ivy
gathered breathing under the shade,
we are always leaving the Paleolithic.

There October exists nameless,
there blankets are skins earned through spilled blood,
there muscled men select and sort with grunts.

Buying ripeness satisfies nothing,
better that fruits be gathered,
by our labors under blue skies.

The crumbling farm of my grandparents carries on,
tired goats grazing dry grass,
tired chickens pecking aimlessly at shadows.

Elsewhere a factory churns ceaselessly,
your head on my chest
everything fibrous, stretching and fraying.

Note: While looking for a translation, I worried about taking good poetry and ruining it or being distracted by cognates. I finally settled on Russian, with the deceptive familiarity of its Cyrillic characters. I found three poems by Osip Mandelstam in *qarrtsiluni* (with new translations by Stephen Dodsen) and selected the one. While studying Mandelstam's original (not a line of Dodsen's translation), I was able to detect repeated phrases and line endings, and I suspect that my subconscious couldn't help but interpret those elements as more "traditional" and perhaps even as part of a poem about a couple romantically entangled (perhaps "Sonnet 43" by Elizabeth Barrett Browning). "Leaving the Paleolithic" grew out of that impulse, but it was also influenced by a photograph of Mandelstam from 1914. I felt compelled to explore that couple's love in the context of the massive social and cultural changes sweeping the industrialized world at the turn of the last century. Hearts may repeat their motions, but so do machines.—Marshall Warfield

Don Riggs

READING WRITING RILKE

I can read Rilke in translation, but
I still don't understand. O Orphic voice,
that only flows in German when read out
loud! I don't understand it either. Choice
between images that the inner eye
sees materialize in the temple,
no direct sun shining there from the sky,
only memories of things, so simple,

a pedigree that goes back to childhood:
sun, wind, clouds, grass, the coffee grounds of earth!
And when I read the original,
my voice rings as if it were understood,
though not by my mind. The music gives birth
to a grove in which I am marginal.

Note: I am captivated by Rilke's *Sonnets to Orpheus*, and have them in original/facing
page translations (several different translators, in fact, different books of them). I
read the poems aloud auf Deutsch, read them in the translations, and I write my
own imitations/reactions/translations of what I like about the first line and take it
elsewhere, and things like that.—Don Riggs

if to interpret text is to contain   I have already slipped
—Daniela Elza

Daniela Elza

INTIMATE HARBOUR*S*

in the pinch   of humanity
                    's loud vanity
the existential hole in the heart   grows daily.

trapped in   an inch of exiled darkness
years pass   without awe
                   without loves
                       without gods
life's h*ail*storm scatters   first d*reams*
truths get im*paled* on another
                   's   astute par*lance*
*drown in the th*ought *of y*our *own diminishing.*

and you *forge*t   the vo*ice* of   rustling rivers

the gentle blue features of
           what you loved
                 what loved you back
without conditions.   between

the woman   dressed in meadow
          the man cloaked in sky

the genius of pure beauty   grips   the mind
at*tempts* to bridge   the void with

a single act of   to *imagine*
              to *translate*
             to *touch*

in that small temple   between two
    before the *demo*lition crew   arrives.

it takes an instant   to be seduced   into
the invisible   the wholeness   of you

the idea of you   next   to you
  str*etched* across   the sheets
                                                 unfurled
skin hums   with the still point
                                                      in which

the language
               of the immeasurable   pools.

Notes: 1. For this activity I asked my parents to send me a favorite Russian poem. They sent me a poem by Alexander Sergeyevich Pushkin. I have had a few close calls with Russian in school and my studies in English Philology. I speak Bulgarian. Russian and Bulgarian not only share the Cyrillic alphabet, but a lot of cognates. After I wrote my poem I looked up the source poem and found that it was written in 1825 and dedicated to Anna Petrovna Kern. I also read a couple of English translations at that time which severely shrank the emotional landscape in which I felt I was immersed while working on my faux translation.
2. The phrase "drown in the thought of your own diminishing" comes from a poem in *thirsty* by Dionne Brand.—Daniela Elza

TRANS/LATE

tonight   I sleep with   text   that   runs away
with itself.   perhaps   it is indecent to   say

what it means.   tangled in   translations.
it is late.   and trains of thought demand a schedule
running back   and forth.   in light of virtual

screen   there is trouble with   line- breaks.
while   unknowing   to know.   to make out
what is   contained.   to sleep   on bony spines of

what is barely conceived.   handwritten.
ink fresh.   how to edit   what is   just found?
curled.   still   dreaming.

what are we doing   here? in seriffed rows
with aisle seats.   looking over each other's shoulder.
each muse.   composed.   sentinels

line the stage.   permit only hand gesture   mime
body language.   and can body   speak.
are we   sitting   too close?

mum's the   word   that can   make
even the greenest technology   sound dirty.

there will be fines   for notes passed between audience.
Ex*it* signs blink to distraction.   such is the ambience.

if to interpret text is to contain   I have already slipped
on test   on invocations   on invitation
on ocean rocks. (did someone call for that ambulance?)

to regain containment   is not being   upright.
is not   making out   and away   with shadow of
poem   still clinging —against   such odds—

a language I can sound   but cannot read.   are we
on the same page   yet?
        this is hardly distressing.

shall I collect these poems?   what to do   with their
echo-   locutions   their eco-
        logical strive?

perhaps true test for poem   is   back in ocean
what still scans   despite dissolution.

did this begin   with   tossing a rock
        in such notions?

this language is   now   sounding me.

what of intimacy   then?   what test for that?
perhaps the music we are   is
        the arc of falling

the page—   a litmus   for what   could be
.easily error.   .stomped.   .in fear of.
.mistaken motive.   .perceived   lack of.

tonight   sleep   with your head in lap of *pretext.*
run fingers along spines of books   you offer
to hold   for me.   such tenderness

to ask   who is here?   who is   barely met.
vaguely glimpsed.   who carries these thoughts

across your thresholds   of metaphor.   listen
to how they   .windchime.   .recombine.

and what of intent?   let rain run its fingers
through intent   and dissolve.   let the train in the distance

rattle out   its questionable logic.

it only runs   in two directions.
and this exchange has already missed
its night   stop.
                is already condemned.

and *wanted*   posters   for its arrest
                 cranked out   on a letter press.

Laurel Hostak

TRINITY (TRANSLATION, VALLEJO)

x

x   x

Have you ever
crossed your eyes and looked up at the stars
until they splinter out in points and edges
exes, crosses
distant and flat?
When we were kids
we used to play
connect-the-dots
with the heavenly bodies,
inventing new constellations:
        Dragon Castle Princess Spaceman

There are fewer stars here,
more artificial light.
Not much to guide me back
to mountains, lakes, and you.
Some days I stretch my limbs
across short distances
and imagine I'm reaching over
deserts, grasslands, floods, and foothills,
my hands just near enough
to graze against your toes.
Some days I feel truncated,
with pieces hacked off and scattered:
one third here
one third there
one third asleep
watching the sun sink
behind glass, rock, and eyelids,
waiting for the Spaceman

to twinkle faint and low.
When he emerges
(as he must, I'm certain),
I'll seize his ankles
and let him carry me,
only to rest in a heap
at your feet.

There are children somewhere
painting faces and fruit in the sky
in hurried strokes
like it's a canvas at their fingertips
and one day
they will understand
distance is everything.

we used to play
connect-the-dots
    —Laurel Hostak

13.
The Rules Poem

The rules poem is a type of list poem that offers a collection of do's and don'ts or a set of directions. These might be rules for treating you or someone else right. They might be rules for best behavior on the subway, at the breakfast table, in the doctor's office, at work, or at a party. Write your rules in the imperative mood. Your rules might be cranky, comic, serious, arch, wacky, realistic, or surrealistic.

Your lines can be of any length. While a rules poem could be rhymed and it could adhere to a fixed meter or per-line syllable count, you might be better off avoiding those constraints. On the other hand, you might take advantage of other organizing principles. You might number your rules or stick to a round number like ten. Try using anaphora, that is, the repetition of a word or group of words at the beginning of each line. Using repetition will lend some shape and organization to your list, but breaking your usual patterns every so often is also a good idea.

The idea of the to-do or not-to-do list goes back all the way to the Ten Commandments and probably before, but here's a less ancient example. This repressive list has been attributed to a Sacramento teachers' contract, although no one seems to know its exact provenance. The list appears widely on websites, and elementary school teachers say they found it reproduced in their education textbooks. This document, while not intended to be a poem, is a provocative model for a list poem.

1915 Rules for Female Teachers

1. You will not marry during the term of your contract.
2. You are not to keep company with men.
3. You must be home between the hours of 8 p.m. and 6 a.m. unless attending a school function.

4. You may not loiter downtown in ice cream stores.

5. You may not travel beyond the city limits unless you have the permission of the chairman of the board.

6. You may not ride in a carriage or automobile with any man unless he is your father or brother.

7. You may not smoke cigarettes.

8. You may not dress in bright colors.

9. You may under no circumstances dye your hair.

10. You must wear at least two petticoats.

11. Your dresses must not be any shorter than two inches above the ankle.

12. To keep the schoolroom neat and clean, you must: sweep the floor at least once daily, scrub the floor at least once a week with hot soapy water, clean the blackboards at least once a day, and start the fire at 7 a.m. so the room will be warm by 8 a.m.

You might create a rules poem such as "What Not to Say to Me at the Class Reunion," "What Not to Do on My Birthday," or "How to Be My Boss."

CLASSROOM IDEA: RULES FOR STUDENTS AND TEACHERS

If you teach grade school, for example fifth grade, have your students list their "Rules for Fifth Graders." Your students will probably come up with hilarious rules. You, as a teacher, might write "Rules for Parents," singling out some egregious examples of helicoptering.

Jim Ellis

HOW TO WRITE A DUBSTEP SONG

If you expect to make me dance
-begin with a simple kick snare
(boom, ba-ch, boom boom ba-ch)
-Enter the synth melody line
(WEEoooWEEEEooooaaaHHHHHHH)
Repeat
-Now add a dissipating cymbal splash
(pshhhhhhhh......)
-cut the drums
-lower register melody
(DO do, bum bum, do DO do
-Fade in a woman's cut up voice
(aaaaaAAAAAeeeeeeOOOooooo)
-Rising bass drum tempo
(Dum Dum Dum Dum dumdumdumdum)
D-D-D-D-D-D-D-D-DROP the Bass

Blythe Davenport

THREE WAYS TO PLAY GHOST
IN THE GRAVEYARD

I. Traditional

We start when it's dark with the bright pop of bubble gum
in a dish, how many pieces do you wish? One foot in the grave
makes you ghost.

II. Flashlight

If the ghost finds you,
she swallows your light
and you become
a ghost too.

III. Storyteller
It starts in with its resonant voice: *I was down by the pond*
when the water started to rise like words in my throat.
And all the spirits scurry for the road, piking it
to beat the flood. *I was standing in the field, a drunk man*
gulping the words air and escape. Its friends' feet creep back,
test each step for dry land as it blows the last of its breath.

Marie Kane

WHAT NOT TO SAY TO ME NOW THAT I AM CRIPPLED

Try not to tell me to *take your time* when holding the door; if I could lag
      behind by choice, I would (sluggishness is not an option with MS)
          and I do appreciate that my sometimes

blind left eye discerns your kind face ignoring my conspicuous left foot
      drop, and that *do good* is your mantra, but refrain from
          suggesting that my walking will improve

if I comply with these cures: a hysterectomy, or its opposite—
      pregnancy, endure the repeated sting of honeybees, or sip
          Aloe Vera juice at a bank-account-emptying spa

at Versailles—any of which ought to turn my question mark spine into
      an exclamation point. Should I ask for a bathroom never, ever tell
          me that I can wait. And for the life of me,

when I relate recent successes, don't cry out "Good for you!" (as if I
      were five and had just learned how to tie my shoes)—when I walk,
          stand, or stay awake ("Good for you!")—

or drive my car to physical therapy ("Good for you!")—or shower by
      myself ("Good for you!")—publish a book of poetry, ("Good
          for you!") drop nothing that day ("Good for you!")—and

when you spy me on my motorized scooter, don't saunter by and claim
      sotto voce to my husband, "I need that more than she does," nor
          should you whisper that your mother, father, sibling,

neighbor died of MS, then tell me that I look Fantastic! Delightful!
      Splendid! Your flood of words insists that I am a marvel; my
          doctors say I am doing well, considering.

Melika Riley

RATCHET 101

It's easy to be ratchet. Follow me!

1) Hold all the confidence and courage in the world (pretty much pretend you're a white person).

2) Look in the mirror and repeat the mantra, "Today is your day. Nobody will fuck with you. Not the rude lady on the bus. Not the grandma who expected you to open the door for her. Not the police or any law enforcing ruler."

3) If a fine ass female or male walks your way, shout to the heavens so everyone can hear you telling that fine ass female/male how sexy they are. Ain't no shame in your game. You're only complimenting them. They should take it and be enamored by your gesture.

4) When you see the fine ass female or male walking your way, make sure to grab their hand and pull them your way to ensure their attention. Who cares about their space right?

5) Don't care about anyone's regards. Remember, your regards always come first.

6) Headphones? Who needs them! Blast your music so everyone can hear it because they need to know how fire your mixtape is. Little did they know, they needed you. You are the DJ of their lives, bumping Cardi B, Drake, and Lil Pump. You're literally blessing their ears.

7) Start issues with people. Who they are, it doesn't matter. If they speak a different language than you or look like they don't match what's downstairs, THEY CAN STILL GET THESE HANDS. If they have the audacity to stand up for themselves, batter up and get in their face. Being in their face says, "Hey! You're different, so get your shit in check. You're going to swing, sir/madam, if I am pushed too far" (objective).

8) Filter your conversation in a professional setting?! Why? They can't tame the wild free beast that is you! Make sure everyone knows who you're talking about and how badly you're going to fuck that person up.

9) When you see a fight or partake in a fight, make sure someone or you is recording the fight. If it doesn't end up in The Shade Room, then you aren't doing anything right. After this, you prepare an iOS press release on Instagram, Facebook, or the Huffington Post giving a backhanded oblivious apology. (Bonus points if the police don't come after you, but your professional life may take a damage.)

10a) Don't forget the dramatized gestures. Nothing gets your point across like rolling your eyes with a twitch and some neck action to assert your dislike; also, clapping your hands in someone's face to let them know you about to put the paws on them.

10b) However, if you want to appear more coy while exhibiting the same amount of ratchetry as 10a, you'll need to adjust the dramatized gestures. You have to keep the right amount of entitlement and aggressiveness while calling on your inner 6-year-old to bring out them crocodile tears. Boo-hoo-hoo until people forget that you caused the situation to occur.

11) Last, but not least, never ever be apologetic about your ratchetness. Keyword: Commitment.

14.
The Superhero Poem

Gods and demigods, the superheroes of myth and legend, have provided people with drama, wisdom, moral lessons, and hopes of divine intervention for thousands of years. Thunderbolt throwers like Zeus and Thor, fierce beauties such as Athena and Artemis, super-mortals like Hercules, not to mention countless deities and folk heroes from other world traditions may be seen as the forerunners of Superman, Batman, Zena Princess Warrior, Wonder Woman, and the rest of the comic book pantheon. Anthropologists tell us that the transcendent, that sense of unearthly force, is a universal feature of human perception or imagination. Today's supernatural pop-cultural good guys and bad guys tie into our attraction to the transcendent. You do not have to be a comic book writer, movie producer, or video game developer to call on a superhero to make extra-normal things happen. You can write a superhero poem.

Write a poem about a superhero who excites your imagination. This might be a character who comes to your rescue or the rescue of others. The character might restore justice, overpower evil doers, or make the world a better place. On the other hand, the superhero might cause trouble. The character might accomplish amazing feats or more modest feats. You can write about a traditional figure from myth or contemporary pop culture, or you can invent your own superhero.

Jeannine Hall Gailey

FEMALE COMIC BOOK SUPERHEROES II:
WHEN CATHOLIC SCHOOL GIRLS STRIKE BACK

In one moment, the cluster of plaid
uniforms, fists and ankles,
descend on the now-hapless criminal:
a horde of angry green bees.

When later interviewed, one girl stated: "Our parents were real proud."

Imagine every girl that walks alone
down a dark alley filled
with her own avenging angels:
feathers flying, fury like dust cudgels.

DIRGE FOR A VIDEO GAME HEROINE: ON DYING AGAIN

It should get less painful, over time—
death by drowning, death by demon bite—
but it doesn't. And each time there is that moment
of melancholy accorded to me by my creator,

the moment my limbs collapse around me,
hair, in a long braid, falling, coiled, at last,
the moment I sigh or let out a choked, guttural "Urghhh…"
depending on whether I was drained of blood

by an undead creature or shot off a cliff
and then the scene around me fades to black.
It is my job, after all, kill or be killed
along with changing outfits unseen between levels,

(kimono? catsuit? chain mail minidress?)
nimbly switching from blade to Uzi,
slaying assailants with increasing speed and accuracy.
And twenty seconds later (mourning period over)

I am back, ready to die again on the whim of the joystick.
One moment, able to somersault over mummies
and scramble between swinging axes; the next, unable
to extract myself from the poisonous slime pit, and so

the last you'll see of me is my mouth making its "O" of surprise,
my eyes closing as if to sleep—this time, maybe, forever.

Samuel Cook

POWER FANTASY

School had long since become intolerable.
No friends, uncountable enemies.
No justice for her there.
Each day, like each harassment,
simply bleeds into the next—
her teeth grind just a little harder,
the slow boil of her stomach builds just a little more.

Home had been her escape from school,
a comfort in pretended ignorance,
until the air finally soured at the dinner table
with the weight of her mother's worried look.
Her father asks her how her day was,
his eyes darting over bruises, splotches, little cuts—
his eyes darting back to hers.
She says her day was fine and asks the same of him.
He tells her it was fine, and that's the last they speak for the night.

But then, by chance, comes an escape from home:
an all-consuming strength wells up within her!
No limit to her limbs, and nothing in her way.
A new world of spandex and kevlar,
adventure and justice.
No shortage of super people who want to know her.
She saves a group that want her—need her.
Young people like her,
desperate to lose themselves in heroism
until the moonlight runs out.
Against all odds,
she can see them soon becoming friends.

…Alas, each turn of the sky brings another school day.
She manacles her muscles and her temper.

She manages her mouth and curious eyes,
fading as far as she can into the background.
Fading as far as she can out of herself.
It doesn't help, of course.
It never has.

As afternoons roll into evenings,
she lets the chains slacken some.
Always, her father asks after her day,
but now she only glares at him from darkened eye sockets,
just to see what would happen.
Nothing.
He says nothing, does nothing,
just returns to the half-burnt salmon and cold asparagus.
Something in her is boiling over.

Out once more in costume, she lets loose, chasing villains.
Things happen quickly, and she goes a bit too far—
breaks one of them—
She goes a bit too far, and her friends rein her in.
Her mask is slipping, and she knows they can see.
Her mask is slipping, and she starts looking for an escape.

I've seen you waiting, standing side-by-side in alphabetical order...
—Janice Dawson

15.
Unanswerable Letter

Write a poem in the form of a letter to someone or something unable to reply. You might address the poem to a family member who has died, a pet, an abstract idea, a physical object. The unanswerable letter prompt could serve as theme, strategy, or both. This approach taps into the occasions of many varieties of poems, including some that are elegiac in tone. Emily Dickinson's "This is my letter to the World" (#441) is a familiar example. Consider using real letters or parts of real letters in your poems.

Emily Dickinson

THIS IS MY LETTER TO THE WORLD (#441)

This is my letter to the World
That never wrote to Me -
The Simple News that Nature told -
With tender Majesty

Her Message is committed
To Hands I cannot see -
For love of Her - Sweet - countrymen -
Judge tenderly - of Me

Karen Chase

FEDERICO FELLINI'S BIRTHDAY

Today, Mom, you would have been 90 and I
Wonder what kind of old woman you
Would have become because when you died
You were young.

I never knew 'til now that
You and Fellini shared
A birthday. You'd both be surprised
How the world's changed. Dad's okay.

His wife, who is younger than me by far, is
Traveling soon to India and we, my husband
Whom you barely knew and I, will stay
With Dad while she's away.

You'd be amazed how small
The world has become. There's so much
To say – I have grandchildren – for one.

If you could see Ruby Leah,
Named after you, you'd
Die again, but this time
Of happiness.

Heather H. Thomas

LETTER MY FATHER NEVER SENT ME

It stinks of decay and something dead there. This place is decadent and morbid in certain ways. It may be beautiful and peaceful, but I like my beauty alive. The other I can understand, but damned if I want to live with it.

All those years you were just across the bridge. You had a new father, new name. Why interfere? How could I, having failed to give your mother a cent.

One day I was flying radar out of Leyte; the next, hoping for a big ship like a C-54, maybe a trade run from New York to Brazil to Africa on up to England and back.

You're going somewhere, and you don't fly yourself into the booby hatch. Which I did, metaphorically speaking, on the 7:17 from Grand Central to Mamaroneck after three martinis.

I couldn't hold still for those ad jobs. Look, there's a war going on. People getting killed by the hundred thousand, guys sweating it out learning life, death and God in the air and in hellholes far worse than New Guinea. And they're learning so they'll never forget.

You get religion in this racket. You get it so you know what it's for. You thank God plenty for letting you sometimes pray a ship in. So when you walk into a church you really see the church for the first time, even though you know God isn't some vast bearded old guy sitting up there on a throne beyond the sky.

I was always happy around water and boats. Nothing holds still except those years on the ship. I would have remembered you then, before you were born. As for airplanes, I am a bit fed up with them.

Look, I can drop in some time. It's easy from here. Try to get some scotch. See if you can get some Canadian ale. Also, see if you can get some salami. I'm nuts about salami and rye bread.

Janice Dawson

DEAR CLASSIC BOOKS I HAVEN'T READ YET

I've seen you waiting, standing side-by-side in alphabetical order by author's last name. Straight spines bound in leather, endpapers swirling, your inner leaves hoping to be judged by your covers' beauty. Other hardbacks stand at attention, thick and heavy, and paperbacks lean to fill the empty spot on the shelf where one was chosen. You all stand together, waiting, waiting for me to make the first move.

I don't blame you. It must be hard to be silent with so many words locked within. Sometimes, when I walk through the library stacks alone, I think I hear whispers and wordplay. I know that you are plotting to lure me in with a meaty theme or seduce me with your rising and falling action. Some of you with loose tongues (or audio features) want to share your entire story, word by word. Others are casually casting a first line for me to catch—

"Last night I dreamt I went to Manderley again."

"It was a bright cold day in April, and the clocks were striking thirteen."

"A throng of bearded men, in sad-colored garments and gray, steeple-crowned hats, intermixed with women, some wearing hoods, and others bareheaded, was assembled in front of a wooden edifice, the door of which was heavily timbered with oak, and studded with iron spikes."

"Whether I shall turn out to be the hero of my own life, or whether that station will be held by anybody else, these pages must show."

"It was the best of times, it was the worst of times...."

"It is a truth universally acknowledged, that a single man in possession of a good fortune, must be in want of a wife."

The other night I dreamed that you, unread novels, all stepped up to the library podium. The first one introduced itself, "Call me Ishmael" and the second one told of a nearly 24-hour odyssey and yes, yes, dozens of pages of stream-of-consciousness narrative technique. Tempting, and I've always hoped to read that one, but I will definitely need some professorial help. The last one spoke in French, "Longtemps, je me suis couché de bonne heure." Seems like a simple beginning, but it may be the most difficult read of all, even in English. Then Emma called me on my cell phone and invited me to a picnic on Box Hill. That's when I woke up.

I know that you only want to create a relationship with a reader to give yourself meaning, to impart the nature of knowledge and existence. Someday soon I will succumb to your beckoning. I'll hold you in my lap and let your words envelop me. Only time will keep us apart.

Sincerely,

Your Future Reader

16.
Write What You (Don't) Know

Create a scene or setting for a play that has not yet been written.

The idea here could be to imagine a play that only now can be written (by you, by anyone) for some reason. It could be a kind of *if* game: What if Chekhov were alive today and wrote a play about aliens invading the Earth (or insert your own contemporary or outlandish scenario here).

This quite naturally brings together disciplines, such as drama, art, and poetry. Not that you actually want to forget or ignore what you know, but fearlessly using and practicing with your imagination to create something wholly new—at least to you—may help you to explore new patterns and themes.

Valerie Fox

PROPERTY PLOT FOR *THE VOYEUR'S HANDBOOK*

On Stage:
Persian carpet with scattered papers, film canisters labeled luck and perseverance, dictionary circa 1900, battery installation instructions (for galvanism, variable number of dry cells)

Cushions, silk, lipsticks (Mimi's)

...Puberty...Petticoats

Side table with inspirational calling cards
water glass (Mr. Fodor), teacup (Mr. Michelin)
scotch tumbler (Mr. Petersen)

Ice cream cone vouchers, ice cream, sherbet
sorbet, tinsel for festive
decorative bird nests

Off Stage:
5-iron
Paints, orange, tangerine, tangelo
Natural light (gates of hell)
Starlings, Devils (Mimi)
Odorous roses—new names, new types
The City

Personal:
Static cling, silk, Dalí's
trademark dripping clock
Scars
Acids

Sibling
rivalry
Lipsticks mirror
Greyhound bus ticket (s)
Notebook and pen (Doctor)

The Fool, The Flood, The World

Joanna Fuhrman

GROUND PLANS FOR A NEW THEATER

#1
The audience is given blindfolds. Inside each blindfold is a picture of a happy family sitting on a yellow couch under a sign that reads "smile."

On the other side of each blindfold, the surface reflects: a bendable mirror only the actors will see.

#2
Behind the set of the boho-chic kitchen, with its teal walls, raw beams and patinaed copper piping, is another set: a different kitchen.

If the audience leaves, the back wall opens to reveal: peeling mustard-color enamel sinks, authentic Brooklyn cockroaches, toaster ovens bursting with crumbs, and an actor asleep (dreaming?) in a foldable chair.

#3
The main dining room of the Love Boat has been recreated with almost perfect verisimilitude.

The only difference is the actresses' breasts, which are not made of the original silicone, but constructed of flesh itself, which will (should) pulsate when (if) an actress chooses to breathe.

John Vick

TRANSIT

Alison screams
Brian! Brian!
beating on the driver side door
while Devon yanks
on the passenger side. She's screaming
at the figure of a body
that doesn't move. Devon says
how they've got to get him
out of here. And
how much did he drink? And
don't they have his roommate's cell
number?
Alison says, No.
She just met him last
week in postmodern lit. Faraway
voice Luke yells, Stella!
Stella! Searching
for her he met earlier
that night, the girl who
said she'd hook-up with him. Who
was totally into him. Who
wouldn't let him down.
Luke yells, then an echo effect ...
Alison's screams interlope ...
... Stella! Brian! Brian! Stella!
A police officer ushers away
the arguing boy. Brian says,
he wasn't doing anything
wrong he was just
sleeping.
An officer tells
Brian he was intoxicated
and in his vehicle

with the keys in the ignition.
Brian says He
thinks the officer could use an education
that the officer doesn't know shit.
The other officer tells him
he's got 35
years of education
meeting the likes of him
and how he's under arrest.
They drive away with Brian, lights
on, no
siren. Allison
and Devon are quiet watching
the tow truck
hauling
Brian! Brian!'s
car down the street.
Luke calls more
and more distant, Stella!
Stella!

Susan Smith Nash

RESCUE CHIMP / RESCUE HUMAN: JANIS CARTER'S LIFE AS A CHIMPANZEE

This play is based on the true story of Lucy, the chimpanzee raised in Norman, Oklahoma by Maurice Temerlin, the former chair of the Psychology Department at the University of Oklahoma and his wife, Jane. In an experiment, to see how far one could push species boundaries. They adopted Lucy, the chimpanzee, when she was newborn, and raised her as though she were their biological daughter.

As you might imagine, the experiment went well while Lucy was cute and small. As she gained strength and reached adolescence, the Temerlins could not handle Lucy (or the very real liability she presented) so they decided to send her off to Gambia, to live with other "rescue chimps" on an island in a river. Lucy had never been around chimpanzees, so the Temerlins hired Janis Carter, a graduate assistant at the University of Oklahoma, who had been a play partner of Lucy's, and who had learned American Sign Language along with Lucy, so they could communicate. Janis's job was to take Lucy to Gambia and help her transition to life with fellow chimps.

When they arrived in Gambia, and made their way to Baboon Island, a strange thing occurred. Lucy, who had been raised as a human, had to learn how to be a chimpanzee. Janis, who had played with Lucy as a human playmate, had to help Lucy make the transition to chimp.

How could Janis guide Lucy?

The only way was for Janis Carter, a young, attractive, 20-something from Norman, Oklahoma, to live, think, and behave as a chimpanzee. Because of her compassion for Lucy, she did so. So, for more than two years, Janis lived on an island in the middle of a river in the heart of Gambia, the only human being within a colony of chimpanzees.

It was a weird reversal. The Temerlins had acquired Lucy the chimpanzee to see what would happen if they raised her as a human being.

Now the Temerlins were hiring Janis Carter, a 20-something homo sapiens graduate student, to live, think, and behave as a chimpanzee.

Most people focus on Lucy, the chimp, and the way she lived within the human family.

What was it like for Janis Carter to live like a chimpanzee for two years?

Why would she do it?

What was she like after the two years?

This play explores Janis Carter and her life as a chimpanzee on Baboon Island in the middle of a river in Gambia.

Personal Aside: I grew up in Norman, Oklahoma, during the time when the primate experiments were taking place at the University of Oklahoma. I talked to Roger Fouts, the psychology professor who taught Washoe, Lucy, and other chimps American Sign Language. I talked to him many times when I was a teenager. He liked to hang out at a record shop on Campus Corner, and I often talked Primate Studies with graduate students.

I often wonder if I ran into Maurice Temerlin, his wife, or even Lucy, without realizing it.

The primate research was absolutely over the top at the University of Oklahoma at that time. The south part of campus used to be a naval base during World War II, and the barracks, office buildings, training facilities, and gigantic swimming pools had all been repurposed for use by the university. Only twenty or twenty-five years after the war had ended, the facilities seemed to be from another century; collapsing, peeling paint, and clunky—utterly out of touch with a batik and tie-dye youth movement, but somehow perfect for the original "Occupy" movement that wanted to blow up earlier generations' "eternal verities." Was there any memory whatsoever of the Armory Show and Marinetti's Futurist Manifesto, 50 years before? My guess is that there was none, and even if there had been, there would have been wholesale denial that the two movements and/or mindsets had anything in common. After all, many of the proponents of Futurism and concepts such as the "Art of War" died in the trenches of World War I. The brilliant sculptor Gaudier-Brzeska was one.

This play features Janis Carter as protagonist.

Lucy and the other chimpanzees also play a part.

It takes place over two years—both as flashbacks and flash-forwards. All the scenes take place on the island.

The play consists of Janis, her actions (or lack of them) with the chimps. She also keeps a diary.

Most of Janis's life takes place in a metal cage that has a corrugated tin roof to help keep the monsoon rains off her.

The chimps live on the island. Janis lives in the cage.

17.
At a Crossroads

If you stand at a crossroads long enough, you see a lot of people, things, happenings. What have you seen? Write a list poem of all the passings-by.

This prompt may be an opportunity to explore a particular crossroad or being at a crossroads (a metaphor, perhaps); the writing may explore place, as it interacts with time, people, with memories of taking a walk or being on a path. A list format has a way of encouraging expansiveness.

This prompt was developed by poet and fiction-writer Kirsten Kaschock (*The Dottery, Confessional Sci-Fi: A Primer*). Here, Brenda Bailey ("Couples Holding Hands") and Karen Schauber ("Mongrel") capture the essence of a busy corner, where many stories intersect. Lisa Prince ("less taken") develops her character and story through voice, reminiscent of haibun or flash.

Lisa Prince

LESS TAKEN

dirt
three stones
my bare toes

the dirt wells up between my toes, sprinkles the webbing with fine dust. I scrunch my feet, digging in. grab a pebble and feel its cool against my skin - no bigger than a thumbnail. I think of monkeys. orangutans. visitors to the zoo. we climb fences, with the grass growing higher than our knees, and laugh at the bumblebees stumbling along - fat and laden with pollen, their bellies yellowed like sunshine. out past where we can see is a creek, lousy with trout, though we can never catch one. our fingers and toes numb in the cold, running water. the thick, wet mud slipping between our toes until our feet settle deep. deeper. like the lost city of Atlantis, disappearing into the depths. the sun glinting off of the water, the way it hits windows and skyscrapers - blinding us, until we shield our eyes and look to the trees. grasses. weeds. the empty lot across the street where we once kicked a soccer ball. your father ran over it with his car, yelling at us as though we'd planned to set the street afire with a noise sharp as gunfire. they built condos there last spring, the large dirt movers eating the ground with their insatiable hunger. and me standing there, barefoot, toes dug into the last of our childhood, wondering if you ever looked back.

Karen Schauber

MONGREL

He stands outside the Starbucks at the corner of Portage and Main, a scruffy, disheveled-looking fellow, arm outstretched. His faded NYC cap flipped over remains empty.

The passersby are not generous today. Monday, always a rush.

Pushing out spittle, he smears his fingertips with his pasty white tongue and smoothes the bristles on top of his head. Maybe if he tidies up a bit.

It's that pesky mutt muscling in on his turf. It's back again; an urban ghost.

He takes a kick at it, shooing the critter along, but the miscreant doesn't budge. Smells something awful too.

A woman in a tumble of blonde curl, stoops to drop a few coins in the cap. His arm now fatigued, droops low. He musters an anaemic smile, the spaces, black and melanoid.

The dog is circling, looking for shade, water, grub; comfort. Loose corrugated skin dripping off bone.

Another good Samaritan. Black coffee and banana.

He sinks down along the wall, on the shady side, to feed, legs outstretched, his cap back on his head. Coffee still hot.

The dog too slumps down in the shade. The pavement here is cool against its belly; its panting beginning to slow.

"It's fresh, man," the passerby says, extending the deli-wrapped pepperoni.

Wafts of spice and grease tickle the sinuses as he swipes the bounty under his nose like a fine cigar.

"Here Lucky" he whispers, leaning toward his sidekick. "I ain't gonna forget you none."

Brenda Bailey

COUPLES HOLDING HANDS

- Couples holding hands, sometimes stopping for a kiss

- Addicts whose nod is almost to the ground

- Children running, running

- Houses coming and going

- Cars - some old some new, cars - some loud some rocking

- A&P, Longacre's, Ocean City

- Left but not gone signage

- Grass turns to concrete

- Rosa Bloom's, Teddy Redd's, get your drink on

- Ms. Sis for a baggie of broken pretzels and chips

- Couples holding hands, sometimes stopping for a kiss

18.
Lagniappe

Use these phrases and expressions in poems.

New car smell
Dog-tired
Your Facebook Timeline
Those pickles in the fridge
Read the skies for storms
It's what we call a triple threat

Chairs not fastened
Stage Kiss
A rabbit's fur
The ants at the picnic
The Sky Rocket at the Fair
The last time we danced to the Beatles

Don Riggs

THE LAST TIME WE DANCED TO THE BEATLES

I threw my knee out—not the one I broke
in the bike accident in France, the one
on the other leg, which was jealous
of my favoring the broken leg for so long,
so started acting up to call attention
to itself. It was all early Beatles
the DJ was playing, so vigorous
with the drumline thumping its steady way

underneath the two- and three-part vocals
about holding your hand, or wanting to,
and offering for you to drive my car
under the shining stars and the dark sky
while I just wanted to slow dance with you
as they were softly playing *Yesterday*.

Harriet Levin

DOG TIRED

Just at the absolute moment of heartbreak,
the thud of spirit
lifts me upward
in flying dreams,
soaring in a gust that catches me
in the tipsy swing of its grasp.

Please do not wake me, my T-shirt fluttering,
my hair tousled in air.
All the world's peaks are accessible,
view spilling into view,
pushing open space,
(the blurriness that exhaustion brings)
each red berry within reach,
clusters, in amplitude—

Rina Terry

EBENEZER HOLINESS PENTECOSTAL CHURCH
PRISON CHAPEL VOLUNTEERS

Everything suspect, including
the old lady's hat. Lining torn
out at Front House frisk. No
mercy for those who tote it—
a Bible frayed from overuse.
It's what we call a triple threat
this Father, Son, Holy Spirit
message. Like the Sky Rocket

at the fair, it spreads unwelcome
stunning light in a cesspit,
hopeless   empty   impossible…
Officers' job security threatened:
recidivism overshadowed by
just a moment's heady epiphany.

Anna Strong

BASS HARBOR, MAINE

My grandmother moved here when there was one
paved main street on the whole wooded island
and lighthouses were still the midnight's sun.
Now the Bass Harbor light is silent
and a machine performs the work once done
by my grandfather. A former pilot,
he learned to read the skies for storms, the sea
for waves that could throw ships against the coast:
his was the lifeguard, his was the bright beam
that led them to shore. He deserted his post
only once, for the birth of my father,
and that thunderous black night was his ghost
forever, the ship bearing his brother
crashed on the rocks just as his newborn child
released his first scream to the wind and the wild.

Luray Gross

IT WAS JANUARY

It was January and I was heading home
with the memory of a stage kiss in my right back pocket
and the echo of your arms around my shoulders
the last time we danced to the Beatles, slow dance,
if one can really call that small circle you lead me in a dance.

It was January and a gray-haired man with an Indian accent
drove his Subaru right through the red light as I entered the intersection.
I tried to apply some speed, but knew in a second of smack and spin,
I'd not avoided him after all.

After the witness, after the cop, while I waited for the tow,
my mind was on the evening, on how I'd planned to get back in my car
and drive south to be there to hear my old friend read
from his new book of poems. We knew this would be his last,
and I had already cautioned myself, touch him gently.

Now all the new car smell is gone, and soon it will be a year
since he died. I've yet to wear his soft burgundy vest,
the one thing I took from the table at the memorial gathering.

The events of each day keep receding on your Facebook Timeline,
yours and mine, but those pickles in the fridge, back near the frost line,
they're still the color of envy. The jar still holds the tang of regret.
If you look closely, there's always a little something extra.

Yesterday an ant disappeared when it crossed from red to black
on the checkered cloth we'd spread across the table, and in the woods
I discovered a rabbit's fur could be all that is left of rabbit
after fox strikes or red-tail barrels down.

I used to think that time was a human invention.
I'd learned about layers and studied road cuts on long rides across the state,

but it still came as a surprise to learn there's a clock
in nearly every cell of every living thing.

The Sky Rocket at the fair might have failed inspection, the chairs
not firmly fastened to the splintery floor, but the ticket taker stands
and opens and closes the little gate and lets the riders in.

Most mornings, most afternoons, I get in my car and drive.

CREDITS

INDEX OF POEMS BY AUTHOR

Wilk, Amberlyn.
"Black and Blue"—*Change a Moment in Time* (p. 62); "A Letter to My Rapist"—*The Thank-You Poem* (p. 50)
Williams, Devin.
"Rats"—*Bibliomancy* (p. 74)
Wong, Jacquiley.
"We Forget the Things We Didn't Say"—*Swipe a Line, Find a Title* (p. 37)
Wood, Peter.
"Fibonacci Poem"—*Fibonacci Poem* (p. 26)

ABOUT THE AUTHORS

Valerie Fox's books of poetry include *The Rorschach Factory* (Straw Gate Books), *Insomniatic* (PS Books), and *The Glass Book* (Texture Press). *Bundles of Letters Including A, V and Epsilon* (Texture Press) is a collaborative work with Arlene Ang. *The Real Sky* (Bent Window Books) features writing by Fox and sketches by Jacklynn Niemiec. Originally from central Pennsylvania, Fox has travelled and lived throughout the world, and has taught writing and literature at numerous universities including Sophia University (in Tokyo) and currently at Drexel University (in Philadelphia).

Lynn Levin is the author of the poetry collections *Miss Plastique* (Ragged Sky Press) and *Fair Creatures of an Hour* (Loonfeather Press), both Next Generation Indie Book Awards finalists in poetry, and *Imaginarium* (Loonfeather Press), a finalist for *ForeWord Magazine*'s Book of the Year Award. She is, as well, the translator from the Spanish of *Birds on the Kiswar Tree* (2Leaf Press), poems by Odi Gonzales. Lynn Levin was born in St. Louis, Missouri. Her poems, essays, and translations have appeared in *Rattle, Ploughshares, Michigan Quarterly Review,* and other places. She teaches at Drexel University. Her website is www.lynnlevinpoet.com.

How heavy do I journey on my way—William Shakespeare

CPSIA information can be obtained
at www.ICGtesting.com
Printed in the USA
LVHW091524091019
633689LV00002B/369/P